The Clean-Eating KITCHEN

D0493691

The
Clean-Eating
KITCHEN

LOVE FOOD™

This edition published by Parragon Books Ltd in 2015
LOVE FOOD is an imprint of Parragon Books Ltd

Parragon Books Ltd
Chartist House
15–17 Trim Street
Bath BA1 1HA, UK
www.parragon.com/lovefood

ISBN: 978-1-4723-5802-8

Printed in China

New recipes and food styling by Sara Lewis
Created and produced by Pene Parker and Becca Spry
Photography by Haarala Hamilton

Notes for the reader

This book uses both metric and imperial measurements. Follow the same units of measurement
throughout; do not mix metric and imperial. All spoon measurements are level: teaspoons are assumed to
be 5 ml and tablespoons are assumed to be 15 ml. Unless otherwise stated, milk is assumed to be full fat,
eggs and individual vegetables are medium, and pepper is freshly ground black pepper. Unless otherwise
stated, all root vegetables should be peeled prior to use. Use organic and sustainable ingredients
wherever possible.

Garnishes, decorations and serving suggestions are all optional and not necessarily included in the
recipe ingredients or method. Any optional ingredients and seasoning to taste are not included in the
nutritional analysis. The times given are an approximate guide only. Preparation times differ
according to the techniques used by different people and the cooking times may also vary from those
given. Optional ingredients, variations or serving suggestions have not been included in the
time calculations.

While the author has made all reasonable efforts to ensure that the information contained in this book
is accurate and up to date at the time of publication, anyone reading this book should note the following
important points:
* Medical and pharmaceutical knowledge is constantly changing and the author and the publisher cannot
and do not guarantee the accuracy or appropriateness of the contents of this book;
* In any event, this book is not intended to be, and should not be relied upon, as a substitute for
appropriate, tailored professional advice. Both the author and the publisher strongly recommend that a
doctor or other healthcare professional is consulted before embarking on major dietary changes;
* For the reasons set out above, and to the fullest extent permitted by law, the author and publisher:
(i) cannot and do not accept any legal duty of care or responsibility in relation to the accuracy or
appropriateness of the contents of this book, even where expressed as 'advice' or using other words
to this effect; and (ii) disclaim any liability, loss, damage or risk that may be claimed or incurred as a
consequence – directly or indirectly – of the use and/or application of any of the contents of this book.

CONTENTS

BENEFITS OF A CLEAN DIET

Clean eating means eating foods in their most natural, whole state, thereby maximising their nutritional benefits. In the last ten years, the space supermarkets devote to ready-prepared chilled meals has expanded hugely, and the shelf-life of some so-called 'fresh' foods has been unnaturally extended, but at what cost? Foods often contain long lists of strange-sounding ingredients that are difficult to pronounce, and whose role is unclear. Bread may no longer contain just flour, yeast, sugar, salt and water; it often includes a number of other ingredients. As increasing evidence emerges about the dangers of eating processed food, clean eating tries to side-step the problem by going natural.

Clean eating involves eating cleaner, leaner meats and more fish, low-starch vegetables, vitamin-rich fruits, protein-boosting nuts and mineral-rich seeds. You are encouraged to replace refined carboyhdrates with smart, complex carbs in the form of legumes, pulses and wholegrains, as they take more time to digest, leaving you feeling full for longer while sustaining your blood sugar levels. Clean eating doesn't mean focusing on calorie restriction; it's about enjoying food as close to 'as nature intended' as possible, avoiding refined processed foods and artificial chemicals, flavours and preservatives, and replacing them with foods grown locally, in a sustainable and environmentally-friendly way. You are encouraged to eat foods that are ethically produced, so for example choosing free-range eggs.

The first step is to look at what you buy and get label-savvy. Food packaging can give a false impression of what is healthy, and words such as 'wholegrain', 'reduced-sugar' or 'high-fibre' may not tell the whole story, even when they are printed alongside pictures of fresh vegetables, green fields, waterfalls and well cared for livestock. Turn the packet over and you may be surprised at what is in the food. Ingredients are listed in order, with those included in the largest amount listed first, and the ingredient you expect to come first may be far down the list. Say 'no' to high-fructose corn syrup, hydrogenated oils, mechanically separated chicken, MSG, sodium nitrates and a high salt content.

Cutting out processed food can feel like a big transition, but as with any dietary change, the hardest part is making the decision. You can still enjoy a burger, just choose a home-made one made with good organic lean steak (see page 76); it will taste better than the shop-bought alternatives. This is a sustainable, proactive approach to healthy living that will see you enjoying what you eat and leave you feeling revitalised.

WHAT YOU CAN EAT

The best way to improve your diet is to start cooking your food from scratch – that way you can know exactly what's in it, including the provenance of the ingredients, and how it has been prepared. Fresh food served straight from the oven should contain no nasty chemicals to enhance its shelf life, especially if you use organic ingredients where possible. You may also be surprised to find that it can save you money, particularly when you have to cook for a family.

CHOOSE WHOLEGRAINS

Wholegrains help us to maintain a healthy digestive system and aid good heart health, as the high amounts of soluble fibre help to reduce cholesterol. They are also rich in complex carbohydrates, for a slow and sustained energy release to help reduce tiredness.

Switching from refined white bread to wholemeal is arguably the single best change you can make to your diet. Wheat flour is sold as 'wholemeal' or 'wholewheat', and both refer to the whole grain that is ground, with nothing taken away during milling, leaving you with 75 per cent flour, 23 per cent bran and two per cent wheatgerm. You might also like to try wholegrain spelt or khorasan flour, both of which are ancient varieties of wheat, or brown rice, hemp, quinoa or buckwheat flour for a gluten-free alternative.

Check the label of any flour carefully. What you think is wholemeal may actually be a mix of refined wheat flour and wholemeal flour, or even solely refined flour with whole seeds, grains or flakes added. Flour that is labelled 'brown' or 'wheatmeal' can be refined white flour with 10–15 per cent fine or coarse bran put back in after milling.

Wheat is also available in its wholegrain form as wheatberries, which can be used as a nutty-tasting salad base and make a great alternative to brown rice. Also try cracked or bulgar wheat, which cooks in less time than wheatberries and is a great base for Middle Eastern salads. Enjoy wholegrain couscous or wholewheat pasta as a hot side dish in place of white couscous or pasta. Oats are always sold in their wholegrain form, either as porridge oats, rolled oats or instant oats. They are available as groats, which look similar to wheatberries and can be cooked in the same way. Look out for barley groats and barley flakes, too. When buying rice, choose wholegrain brown rice or coloured rice such as Camargue red rice or black wild rice. White rice not only has the fibre removed, but most of the vitamin B is lost in the processing too. Also choose wholegrain corn or wholegrain cornmeal.

FISH AND MEAT

Fish is rich in protein, vitamin B12, which is vital for a healthy nervous system, and iodine, which the thyroid gland needs to function effectively. Oily fish, such as salmon, trout, tuna, sardines, herring and mackerel, are rich in omega-3 fats, which are thought to have many health benefits, including helping to lower blood pressure. Try to include fish in your diet twice a week, and make one of those portions an oily fish.

Don't be afraid to ask your fishmonger where the fish has come from, how it was caught and whether is it farmed or wild. Look out for the Marine Stewardship Council (MSC) logo, which certifies that the fish has been sourced from well-managed fisheries, where fishing methods minimise environmental impact so we can be confident of healthy fish stocks in the future.

When buying meat and poultry, ask your butcher about its provenance and choose farms with high welfare standards approved by the Soil Association or the RSPCA.

Try to have at least two meat-free days per week, and try to keep portions to no more than 150 g/5$^{1}/_{2}$ oz per person. Trim the fat off meat before cooking and remove the skin from poultry before eating.

FATS AND OILS

We need fat in the diet to help the body to absorb fat-soluble vitamins A, D, E and K and to provide essential fatty acids. The Mediterranean diet, rich in olive oil, has long been considered to be healthy, but there is now a wide range of other cold-pressed oils such as hemp, avocado and nut oils, available in some supermarkets. They are traditionally made without the use of chemicals or solvents, and at temperatures below 40°C/104°F, which ensures the full character and essence of the oil is preserved, with natural variations in character and appearance from season to season. Nearly all cold-pressed oils are a natural source of vitamin E, which is an important cancer-fighting antioxidant, plus they contain essential fatty acids 3 and 6. Many cold-pressed oils, such as flaxseed and walnut oils, keep less well than refined oils, so buy them in small quantities and keep them in a cool place or in the refrigerator.

Butter contains saturated fat, so use it sparingly. Make dips and dressings with yogurt rather than shop-bought mayonnaise. The British Dietetic Association recommends that an average man should consume only 30 g/1 oz saturated fat per day and women 20 g/$^{3}/_{4}$ oz per day.

FRUIT AND VEGETABLES

We are all encouraged to eat five portions of fruit and vegetables every day, but how many of us do this? A medium fruit, such as an apple, pear or banana, counts as one of your five a day, as does two kiwi fruit or plums or seven strawberries. Potatoes don't count, but sweet potatoes and other starchy vegetables do. While fresh is generally considered best, frozen fruit and vegetables can sometimes contain more vitamins and minerals than fresh, plus they have the benefit of being convenient and are ideal for smoothies and compotes. Canned tomatoes or pulses such as haricot or red kidney beans in water make a great store-cupboard standby and count towards your five a day.

Try to choose organically-grown by traditional crop rotation methods using natural pesticides and fertilisers from your local farmers' market or pick-your-own farm. Some supermarkets also support local producers and will label food accordingly. Alternatively, why not have a go at growing your own? You don't need a large garden, just convert the end of a flower bed or grow salad leaves in tubs, or have a hanging basket of strawberries by the back door. There's something immensely satisfying about harvesting your own food, and it's a great way to encourage children to be more interested in where their food comes from.

Most pesticides on the surface of fruit and vegetables can be removed with thorough washing. Choose unwaxed lemons, but buy them in small quantities as the wax contains a fungicide to prevent mould growth.

UNREFINED SUGARS

Most of us eat far too much sugar, and with obesity levels rising it is good to review what you eat. Rather than grabbing a chocolate bar packed with chemically derived sugars for a quick fix, go for a home-made cookie with protein-boosting nuts and wholemeal flour and smaller amounts of flavourful dark muscovado sugar for a more sustained energy boost (see page 116). Most people love moist dark chocolate brownies, but cut down on refined sugar and fat by adding cooked dates (see page 106). Naturally sweet beetroot makes a surprising addition to a rich chocolate cake (see page 102), and mean you don't need quite so much butter or sugar. If using sugar, choose types that are as unrefined as possible; naturally brown muscovado or palm sugar work well, but check the packet to make sure the sugars aren't coloured after manufacture. Maple syrup adds a delicate natural sweetness, but again it may not be all that it seems – check the label as some brands are mixed with high-fructose corn syrup. Locally-produced runny or set honey tastes delicious, and a small spoonful goes a long way.

KEEP IT SIMPLE

This book is all about going back to good, home-cooked meals. Gone are the days of the ready meal, the packet of ready-made pastry or the jar of pasta sauce. But that doesn't mean supper will take you an age to prepare and cook, or that you need to go on a cookery course. The recipes in this book are simple, approachable and made with raw, natural ingredients that are easy to find in your favourite supermarket, health food shop or farmers' market, and they taste great! Here are just some of the problems you can help avoid if you switch to clean eating.

High salt intake – even if you don't add salt to your food, you may still be consuming far too much of it if you eat processed foods such as breakfast cereals, canned soups, ready-sliced bread and packet sauces, not to mention crisps, peanuts and other snacks. An excessive intake of salt can cause a rise in blood pressure, risk of stroke and heart disease and kidney failure. The World Health Organisation recommends that adults should eat no more than 6 g of salt a day. Most adults eat in excess of 9 g, and the figure is much higher for those who eat lots of junk food and ready meals. Every cell in the body needs salt to regulate fluid balance and maintain healthy blood pressure, but the amount required is small and varies according to age, climate and physicality.

High fructose levels – health workers fear that the high level of fructose in our diet is set to become as great a problem as our alcohol consumption. We consume over three times more fructose than we did 50 years ago. The liver can usually metabolise the amount of fructose that is found naturally in fruits and vegetables, but can struggle with the amounts now added to processed foods, particularly in the form of high-fructose corn syrup. Overload the body over a long period of time and the liver may become enlarged. You won't necessarily look fat if you are over-consuming fructose. Avoid sugary processed foods and fruit juices, and fizzy drinks with little or no added nutritional benefit. It is also wise to avoid sweeteners, apart from some plant-based ones.

High trans fats consumption – these are naturally found in meat and dairy products, but are also artificially produced to go into some biscuits and cakes, with edible oils being industrially hardened to ensure they stay solid at room temperature. It is the artificially made trans fats that should be avoided. Research indicates there is a link between high consumption of these and high cholesterol levels and heart disease.

TAKING STOCK

Forget about using salty stock cubes, it's very easy to make your own stock. Once it is cooked, leave it to cool, then pour it into plastic containers or ice-cube trays to freeze in handy-sized amounts so that it is ready and waiting when you need it. Just defrost in the microwave in minutes, or in the refrigerator overnight, before use.

VEGETABLE STOCK

Put a quartered onion, with just the outer layer of skin removed, in a medium saucepan. Add three thickly sliced carrots, two thickly sliced celery sticks, two roughly chopped tomatoes, a bay leaf, two stems of fresh rosemary or thyme, the stems from a small bunch of fresh parsley and the green tops of two leeks. Season with a little sea salt and freshly ground black pepper, then pour in 1.4 litres/2½ pints water. Bring to the boil, then partially cover with a lid and simmer for 1 hour. Leave to cool, then strain through a sieve.

CHICKEN STOCK

Strip the meat from a chicken carcass left over from a roast chicken, cover and chill in the refrigerator. Put the carcass in a large saucepan. Add a quartered onion, with just the outer layer of skin removed, two thickly sliced carrots, two thickly sliced celery sticks and a handful of fresh herbs. Season with a little sea salt and freshly ground black pepper, then pour in 1.4 litres/2½ pints water, or more if needed to completely cover the carcass. Bring to the boil, then partially cover with a lid and simmer for 1 hour. Leave to cool, then strain through a sieve.

BREAKFASTS

Healthy breakfast frittata	20
Spinach scrambled eggs with wholegrain rye toast	22
Mushroom and egg cups with wholemeal toast	24
Baked mushroom and herb ricotta	27
Courgette fritters	28
Buckwheat blinis with pears and blueberries	30
Raw buckwheat and almond porridge	32
Spicy apple oats	35
Cranberry and seed muesli	37
Spelt breakfast rolls with spiced fig conserve	38
Citrus fruit refresher	40
Green jump-start juice	43
Berry kick-start smoothie	44

HEALTHY BREAKFAST FRITTATA

Serve this frittata straight from the pan with home-made wholemeal bread (see page 24), or wrap it in baking paper and foil and enjoy it cold at work.

SERVES: 4   PREP: 15 MINS   COOK: 20 MINS

250 g/9 oz baby new potatoes, unpeeled and sliced
2 tbsp virgin olive oil
4 spring onions, thinly sliced
1 courgette, thinly sliced
115 g/4 oz baby spinach, destalked
large pinch of smoked hot paprika
6 eggs
sea salt and pepper

1 Bring a saucepan of water to the boil, add the potatoes and cook for 5 minutes, or until just tender, then drain well.

2 Meanwhile, heat 1 tablespoon of oil in a large ovenproof frying pan over a medium heat. Add the spring onions, courgette and potatoes and fry, stirring and turning the vegetables, for 5 minutes, or until just beginning to brown.

3 Add the spinach and paprika and cook, stirring, for 1–2 minutes, or until the leaves have just wilted.

4 Preheat the grill to medium–hot. Crack the eggs into a bowl and season with salt and pepper. Beat lightly with a fork until evenly mixed. Pour a little extra oil into the pan if needed, then pour in the eggs and cook for 5–6 minutes, or until they are almost set and the underside of the frittata is golden brown.

5 Grill the frittata for 3–4 minutes, or until the top is browned and the eggs are set. Cut into wedges and serve.

LOVE LEFTOVERS

If you have cooked new potatoes left over from last night's supper in the refrigerator, use these rather than cooking more.

PER SERVING: 241 CALS | 15.1G FAT | 3.5G SAT FAT | 13.7G CARBS | 2.6G SUGARS | 1.1G SALT | 2.9G FIBRE | 13.2G PROTEIN

SPINACH SCRAMBLED EGGS WITH WHOLEGRAIN RYE TOAST

Wholegrain rye bread is packed with fibre, and it has a rich, nutty flavour that complements creamy scrambled eggs perfectly.

SERVES: 4   PREP: 15 MINS   COOK: 15 MINS

200 g/7 oz baby spinach, roughly chopped
8 large eggs
3 tbsp milk
15 g/1/2 oz unsalted butter
4 slices of wholegrain rye bread
pinch of freshly grated nutmeg
sea salt and pepper

1 Place a large frying pan over a high heat. Add the spinach and cook in the water still clinging to it from washing, stirring, for 1–2 minutes or until the leaves have just wilted. Transfer it to a sieve and squeeze out as much of the moisture as possible. Keep warm.

2 Crack the eggs into a bowl, add the milk and season with salt and pepper. Beat lightly with a fork until evenly mixed.

3 Melt the butter in the frying pan over a medium heat. Pour in the eggs and cook, stirring, for 5–6 minutes, or until they are just beginning to set. Add the spinach and cook, stirring, for 2–3 minutes, or until the eggs are lightly set.

4 Meanwhile, lightly toast the rye bread, then cut each slice in half.

5 Spoon the spinach scramble over the toast, sprinkle with nutmeg and serve immediately.

THE RIGHT RYE

Be sure to choose wholegrain rye bread. Check the ingredients list to ensure no refined flour is included.

PER SERVING: 300 CALS | 19G FAT | 6G SAT FAT | 13G CARBS | 1.5G SUGARS | 1.1G SALT | 3G FIBRE | 21G PROTEIN

MUSHROOM AND EGG CUPS WITH WHOLEMEAL TOAST

Enjoy these baked eggs straight from the oven with hot wholemeal toast and baked tomatoes, or pack in foil with cherry tomatoes for a breakfast to go.

SERVES: 6   PREP: 20 MINS   COOK: 20 MINS

2 tbsp virgin olive oil
2 oak-smoked back bacon rashers,
rind removed, diced
115 g/4 oz button mushrooms, sliced
3 eggs
125 ml/4 fl oz milk
40 g/1½ oz Cheddar cheese, grated
1 tbsp finely snipped fresh chives
200 g/7 oz cherry tomatoes on the vine
sea salt and pepper
6 slices of home-made wholemeal bread
(see below), to serve

1 Preheat the oven to 190°C/375°F/Gas Mark 5. Line the holes of a six-hole muffin tin with baking paper. Heat 1 tablespoon of oil in a small frying pan over a medium-high heat. Add the bacon and fry for 2–3 minutes, or until just beginning to turn golden. Add the mushrooms and fry, stirring, for 2 minutes. Spoon the mixture into the muffin tin holes.

2 Crack the eggs into a jug, add the milk, Cheddar and chives and season with salt and pepper. Beat lightly with a fork until evenly mixed, then pour into the holes of the muffin tin. Stir so the bacon and mushrooms are not all on the base of the tin. Bake in the centre of the oven for 15 minutes.

3 Put the tomatoes on a baking sheet, drizzle with the remaining oil and sprinkle with salt and pepper. Add to the oven for the last 10 minutes of cooking time. Lightly toast the bread, then cut each slice in half.

4 Lift out the mushroom and egg cups, arrange on plates with the toast and baked tomatoes and serve immediately.

HOME-MADE BREAD

To make wholemeal bread, follow the Pizza Base recipe on page 70, doubling the quantities of all the ingredients. Press the risen dough into a greased 900-g/2-lb loaf tin and sprinkle with 2 tablespoons of porridge oats. Cover with clingfilm and leave to rise for 30 minutes. Preheat the oven to 220°C/ 425°F/Gas Mark 7 and bake for 25–30 minutes, or until the top is golden and the bottom sounds hollow when tapped. Loosen and leave to cool on a rack.

PER SERVING: 418 CALS | 18.1G FAT | 4.8G SAT FAT | 49.5G CARBS | 3.7G SUGARS | 1.9G SALT | 7.4G FIBRE | 18.8G PROTEIN

BAKED MUSHROOM AND HERB RICOTTA

Ricotta cheese is lower in fat than most cheeses, and is an excellent source of protein and calcium.

SERVES: 4   PREP: 15 MINS   COOK: 15–20 MINS

4 large flat mushrooms
1 tbsp virgin olive oil
1 shallot, roughly chopped
60 g/2¼ oz fresh flat–leaf parsley, roughly chopped
1 tbsp snipped fresh chives
250 g/9 oz ricotta cheese
sea salt and pepper

1 Preheat the oven to 200°C/400°F/Gas Mark 6. Remove the stems from the mushrooms and set aside. Put the mushrooms in a shallow baking dish and brush with the oil.

2 Put the mushroom stems, shallot, parsley and chives in a food processor and process until finely chopped. Season with salt and pepper.

3 Put the chopped ingredients in a large bowl with the ricotta and stir well.

4 Spoon the herb ricotta onto the mushrooms. Bake for 15–20 minutes, or until tender. Serve immediately.

GOES WELL WITH

Home–made spelt rolls (see page 38), plain or toasted, make a good accompaniment to the mushrooms and soak up the tasty juices.

PER SERVING: 86 CALS | 7G FAT | 3G SAT FAT | 49.5G CARBS | 1G SUGARS | 0.1G SALT | 1.5G FIBRE | 5G PROTEIN

COURGETTE FRITTERS

Quick to prepare, these fritters make a filling start to the day. Brown rice flour is a nutritious alternative to wheat flour, and is gluten-free.

SERVES: 5   PREP: 20 MINS   COOK: 40 MINS

85 g/3 oz brown rice flour
1 tsp baking powder
2 eggs, beaten
200 ml/7 fl oz milk
250 g/9 oz courgettes
2 tbsp fresh thyme leaves
1 tbsp virgin olive oil
sea salt and pepper

1 Sift the flour and baking powder into a large bowl, then tip the remaining bran in the sieve into the bowl. Make a well in the centre. Pour the eggs into the well and, using a wooden spoon, gradually draw in the flour. Slowly pour in the milk, stirring continuously to form a thick batter.

2 Meanwhile, place kitchen paper on a plate and grate the courgettes over it so it absorbs some of the juices. Pat the courgettes dry, then add them and the thyme to the batter, season with salt and pepper and mix well.

3 Heat the oil in a frying pan over a medium–high heat. Drop tablespoons of the batter into the pan, leaving a little space between them. Cook in batches for 3–4 minutes on each side, or until golden brown.

4 Line a baking sheet with kitchen paper. Transfer the fritters to the baking sheet using a slotted spoon and let them drain well. Remove the kitchen paper and keep each batch warm while you make the rest. Allow five fritters per person and serve immediately.

SPICE IT UP

These fritters are delicious with a large pinch of dried red chilli flakes mixed in with the salt and pepper.

PER SERVING: 151 CALS | 6.8G FAT | 2G SAT FAT | 16.6G CARBS | 3.5G SUGARS | 1.4G SALT | 1.3G FIBRE | 5.9G PROTEIN

BUCKWHEAT BLINIS WITH PEARS AND BLUEBERRIES

These Russian-style pancakes were traditionally served to mark the coming of spring, and are made with nutritious and nutty-tasting buckwheat flour.

SERVES: 4   PREP: 25 MINS
RISE: 1 HOUR   COOK: 25 MINS

175 g/6 oz buckwheat flour
1/2 tsp sea salt
2 tsp dark muscovado sugar
1 tsp easy-blend dried yeast
125 ml/4 fl oz milk
125 ml/4 fl oz water
1 tbsp virgin olive oil

TOPPING
25 g/1 oz unsalted butter
2 pears, cored and thickly sliced
150 g/5 1/2 oz blueberries
2 tbsp runny honey
juice of 1/2 lemon
200 g/7 oz Greek-style natural yogurt
pinch of ground cinnamon
25 g/1 oz toasted unblanched hazelnuts,
roughly chopped

1 To make the blinis, put the flour, salt, sugar and yeast in a large bowl and mix well. Put the milk and water in a small saucepan and gently heat until just warm, then gradually whisk into the flour until you have a smooth, thick batter.

2 Cover the bowl with a large plate and leave it in a warm place to rise for 40–60 minutes, or until bubbles appear on the surface and the batter is almost doubled in size.

3 Heat half the oil in a large griddle pan over a medium heat. Remove the pan from the heat briefly and wipe away excess oil using kitchen paper. Return the pan to the heat and drop dessertspoons of the batter into it, leaving a little space between them. Cook for 2–3 minutes, or until the undersides are golden and the tops are beginning to bubble.

4 Turn the blinis over with a spatula and cook for 1–2 minutes more. Transfer them to a baking sheet and keep warm in the oven while you make the rest. Continue wiping the pan with oiled kitchen paper between cooking batches.

5 To make the topping, melt the butter in a frying pan over a medium heat. Add the fruit and cook for 2–3 minutes, or until hot. Drizzle over the honey and lemon juice and cook for 1 minute, or until the blueberry juices begin to run.

6 Arrange three blinis on each of four plates, top with spoonfuls of the yogurt, the hot fruit, a little ground cinnamon and the hazelnuts. Serve immediately.

GLUTEN-FREE FLOUR

Buckwheat flour is ground from a plant related to rhubarb. It is gluten-free, but check the label as it may be milled by machines used for wheat, making it unsuitable for those on a gluten-free diet.

PER SERVING: 437 CALS | 17.4G FAT | 6.6G SAT FAT | 63.8G CARBS | 26.6G SUGARS | 0.9G SALT | 8.5G FIBRE | 12.9G PROTEIN

RAW BUCKWHEAT AND ALMOND PORRIDGE

This simple no-cook porridge is a great stand-by breakfast that will keep in the refrigerator for up to three days.

SERVES: 6   SOAK: OVERNIGHT
PREP: 45 MINS   CHILL: 30 MINS

70 g/2 1/2 oz unblanched almonds, soaked
in cold water overnight
300 ml/10 fl oz water
350 g/12 oz raw buckwheat groats, soaked in
cold water for 1 1/2 hours
1 tsp ground cinnamon
4 tbsp light agave nectar
125 g/4 1/2 oz strawberries, hulled and sliced, to serve

1 To make the almond milk, drain the almonds and transfer to a blender or food processor. Add the water and process for 1–2 minutes, or until they have broken down as much as possible.

2 Line a sieve with muslin and place it over a large bowl or jug. Pour the almond milk into the sieve and leave to drain for 30 minutes. Squeeze through as much of the liquid as possible; you should get approximately 300 ml/10 fl oz almond milk.

3 Rinse the soaked buckwheat well with cold water. Transfer it to a blender or food processor, add the almond milk, cinnamon and 2 tablespoons of agave nectar and process until slightly coarse. Chill in the refrigerator for at least 30 minutes, or overnight if you have the time.

4 Serve the porridge in small bowls, topped with the strawberries and remaining 2 tablespoons of agave nectar.

ALMOND MILK

Ideal for anyone intolerant of dairy, almond milk makes a great choice for breakfast. Almonds are rich in fibre, vitamins and minerals, so the milk is nutritious as well as delicious.

PER SERVING: 305 CALS | 7.4G FAT | 0.8G SAT FAT | 55.9G CARBS | 9.8G SUGARS | TRACE SALT | 8G FIBRE | 9.4G PROTEIN

SPICY APPLE OATS

Healthy rolled oats get a boost of flavour from apples, dried fruit and cinnamon in this simple cereal. It can be made the day before eating and stored in the refrigerator overnight.

SERVES: 6   PREP: 30 MINS   COOK: 35 MINS

4 red-skinned dessert apples
finely grated zest of 1 unwaxed lemon
and juice of 1/2 lemon
1/2 tsp virgin olive oil, to grease
2 large eggs
150 ml /5 fl oz milk
50 g/1³/4 oz light muscovado sugar
1 tsp baking powder
1/2 tsp sea salt
1/2 tsp ground cinnamon
225 g/8 oz porridge oats
75 g/2³/4 oz dried fruit (raisins, cranberries, cherries, chopped apricots or a combination)
15 g/¹/2 oz unsalted butter

1 Peel, core and roughly chop two of the apples, then put them in a saucepan. Add the lemon zest and juice, cover and cook over a medium-low heat for 5–10 minutes, or until soft. Mash until smooth, then leave to cool.

2 Preheat the oven to 190°C/375°F/Gas Mark 5. Lightly grease a medium, shallow baking dish with oil. Crack the eggs into a large bowl, add the milk and beat with a fork until evenly mixed. Add the apple sauce, sugar, baking powder, salt and cinnamon and stir well. Core and dice the remaining two apples, then add them to the mixture with the porridge oats and dried fruit.

3 Spoon the mixture into the prepared dish. Melt the butter in a small saucepan, then drizzle it over the oats. Bake for 25 minutes, or until bubbling. Leave to cool before serving.

SIMPLY THE BEST OATS

Oats are a wholegrain food and contain protein, B vitamins and vitamin E. Their simplicity is their beauty, and their popularity as a breakfast cereal has grown enormously in recent years.

PER SERVING: 300 CALS | 8G FAT | 3G SAT FAT | 50G CARBS | 26G SUGARS | 0.7G SALT | 5G FIBRE | 9G PROTEIN

CRANBERRY AND SEED MUESLI

A naturally sweetened alternative to ready-made muesli, this nutty and fruity breakfast is bursting with nutrients and is so tasty that no-one in the family will be able to resist!

SERVES: 6
PREP: 15 MINS   SOAK: 1 HOUR

175 g/6 oz porridge oats
60 g/2¼ oz rye flakes
75 g/2¾ oz unblanched almonds, roughly chopped
50 g/1¾ oz dried cranberries
2 tbsp sunflower seeds
2 tbsp pumpkin seeds
2 tbsp flaxseeds
2 crisp dessert apples, cored and coarsely grated
400 ml/14 fl oz freshly juiced apple juice, plus extra to serve

1 Put the oats, rye flakes, almonds, cranberries, sunflower seeds, pumpkin seeds and flaxseeds in a large bowl and mix well. Stir in the apples.

2 Add the apple juice, stir, cover and leave to soak for 1 hour, or chill in the refrigerator overnight.

3 Spoon the mixture into six serving bowls. Serve with a small jug of extra fresh apple juice for pouring over.

PLAN AHEAD

Mix a large batch of the dry ingredients and store in an airtight container for up to four weeks, ready to add apple and apple juice for serving.

PER SERVING: 330 CALS | 13G FAT | 2G SAT FAT | 36G CARBS | 14G SUGARS | TRACE SALT | 8G FIBRE | 9G PROTEIN

SPELT BREAKFAST ROLLS WITH SPICED FIG CONSERVE

What could be nicer than starting the day with home-baked bread?
The quick-cook fig conserve is a great cheat's way to make your own jam at home too.

MAKES: 16 ROLLS AND 500 G/1 LB 2 OZ JAR OF CONSERVE
PREP: 45 MINS   RISE: OVERNIGHT PLUS 50 MINUTES
COOK: 45 MINS

500 g/1 lb 2 oz wholemeal spelt plain flour,
plus extra to dust
1 tbsp dark muscovado sugar
1 tsp sea salt
2 tsp easy-blend dried yeast
2 tbsp sesame seeds, plus extra to sprinkle
2 tbsp sunflower seeds, plus extra to sprinkle
2 tbsp flaxseeds, plus extra to sprinkle
2 tbsp virgin olive oil, plus extra to grease
300–350 ml/10–12 fl oz warm water
1 tsp milk, to glaze
unsalted butter, to serve

SPICED FIG CONSERVE
225 g/8 oz dried figs, diced
3 small dessert apples, peeled, quartered,
cored and diced
finely grated zest and juice of 1 orange
1 tbsp light muscovado sugar
1/4 tsp ground mixed spice
250 ml/9 fl oz water

1 Put the flour, dark muscovado sugar and salt in a bowl and mix well. Stir in the yeast, sesame seeds, sunflower seeds and flaxseeds. Add the oil, then gradually mix in enough warm water to create a soft dough, at first using a wooden spoon, then squeezing together with your hands.

2 Dust a work surface with the spelt flour, then knead the dough for 5 minutes. Return it to the bowl, cover with lightly oiled clingfilm and leave it to rise overnight in the refrigerator.

3 Meanwhile, to make the spiced fig conserve, put the dried figs, apples, orange zest and juice, light muscovado sugar, mixed spice and water in a saucepan. Cover and simmer over a medium heat, stirring from time to time, for 30 minutes, or until thick. Leave to cool. Sterilise a 500 g/1 lb 2 oz jar, then spoon in the conserve and leave until completely cold. Chill in the refrigerator, where it will keep for up to 10 days.

4 Line two baking sheets with baking paper. Dust a work surface with more of the spelt flour. Knead the dough briefly, then cut it into 16 pieces. Roll each piece into a ball, put one ball in the centre of each baking sheet, then arrange the others around it, leaving a little space between them.

5 Cover each sheet with lightly oiled clingfilm and leave to rise in a warm place for 40–50 minutes. Preheat the oven to 220°C/425°F/Gas Mark 7. Remove the clingfilm, brush the rolls with the milk and sprinkle with the remaining seeds. Bake for 15 minutes, or until the rolls are browned and sound hollow when tapped underneath. Serve with butter and the conserve.

TO STERILISE JARS

Preheat the oven to 110°C/225°F/Gas Mark 1/4. Stand the jars on a baking sheet with their lids resting on the top of them and heat in the oven for 30 minutes. Leave to cool before filling.

PER ROLL (NO CONSERVE): 199 CALS | 4.4G FAT | 0.5G SAT FAT | 37.5G CARBS | 13.5G SUGARS | 0.4G SALT | 6G FIBRE | 6G PROTEIN

CITRUS FRUIT REFRESHER

You can quickly put this together in the morning, or make it the night before and chill it in the refrigerator in a sealed plastic container so it's ready and waiting for you.

SERVES: 4 PREP: 20 MINS

1 ruby grapefruit
1 pink grapefruit
2 oranges
1 honeydew melon, halved, deseeded, peeled
and cut into chunks
finely grated zest and juice of 1 lime
25 g/1 oz fresh mint, finely shredded
2 tbsp runny honey

1 Cut the peel and pith away from the grapefruits and oranges with a small serrated knife. Hold one of the fruits above a bowl and cut between the membranes to release the segments. Squeeze the juice from the membranes into the bowl. Continue until the fruits have all been segmented.

2 Add the melon, lime zest and juice and half the mint. Drizzle over the honey, then gently stir with a large spoon. Decorate with the remaining mint and serve.

GROWING MINT

Mint is such a prolific herb that just one packet of seeds in a large flower pot will usually provide enough for the whole summer.

PER SERVING: 170 CALS | 0.5G FAT | 0.1G SAT FAT | 43.6G CARBS | 35G SUGARS | TRACE SALT | 4.9G FIBRE | 2.3G PROTEIN

GREEN JUMP-START JUICE

If you like spinach soup, you will love this juice. You don't get a huge amount of juice from the leaves, but what you do get is concentrated with antioxidants, minerals and vitamins.

SERVES: 1   PREP: 10 MINS

55 g/2 oz baby spinach
25 g/1 oz watercress
1 courgette, halved
2 dessert apples, halved
1 tsp wheatgrass powder (optional)
small handful of ice (optional)

1   Feed the spinach and watercress, then the courgette and apples, through a juicer.

2   Stir in the wheatgrass powder, if using. Half-fill a glass with ice, if using, pour in the juice and serve immediately.

NUTRIENT BOOST

Most of us don't eat enough green veg and this juice is an easy way to increase your consumption. Add to that the highly nutritious wheatgrass powder and you have a great kick-start.

PER SERVING: 223 CALS | 1.3G FAT | TRACE SAT FAT | 51.4G CARBS | 35.6G SUGARS | 0.1G SALT | 1G FIBRE | 6.4G PROTEIN

BERRY KICK-START SMOOTHIE

*This energising, gorgeous-looking smoothie is a delicious
and healthy way to kick-start your day.*

SERVES: 2   PREP: 10 MINS

175 g/6 oz blueberries
115 g/4 oz cranberries
150 g/5 oz natural yogurt
2 tsp clear honey
4 tbsp cold water

1 Put the blueberries and cranberries in a blender and
process until smooth.

2 Add the yogurt, honey and water and process again. Pour
into a glass and serve.

THE BUZZ ABOUT HONEY

Honey supplies energy in the form of simple
carbohydrates, and is a mixture of fructose
and glucose. Sweet foods stimulate the brain to
produce endorphins, the body's natural
painkillers. Agave syrup, brown rice syrup and
date syrup can all be used instead of honey.
Agave syrup is naturally sweeter than honey.
Brown rice syrup has a mild caramel flavour and tastes rather like maple syrup. Date
syrup is a thick, concentrated purée of lightly
cooked dates; you can make it by gently simmering dates with a little water, cinnamon and
vanilla, then puréeing.

PER SERVING: 288 CALS | 5.6G FAT | 3.1G SAT FAT | 57.9G CARBS | 40.5G SUGARS | 0.1G SALT | 9.5G FIBRE | 6.9G PROTEIN

PEA SOUP

This simplest of soups is bursting with fresh summer flavour,
and the salty blue cheese complements the sweet peas.

SERVES: 4   PREP: 20 MINS   COOK: 25 MINS

40 g/1¹/2 oz unsalted butter
2 shallots, finely chopped
1 litre/1³/4 pints home-made vegetable
stock (see page 16)
400 g/14 oz podded peas
60 g/2¹/4 oz crème fraîche
sea salt and pepper
85 g/3 oz blue cheese, such as Roquefort,
crumbled, to serve

CROUTONS

2 slices of home-made wholemeal bread
(see page 24), cut into cubes
2 tbsp virgin olive oil

1 To make the croûtons, preheat the oven to 150°C/300°F/ Gas Mark 2. Toss the bread with the oil and sprinkle with ¹/2 teaspoon of salt and ¹/2 teaspoon of pepper. Arrange the cubes on a baking sheet in a single layer, then bake for 25 minutes.

2 Meanwhile, to make the soup, melt the butter in a large saucepan over a medium heat. Add the shallots and fry, stirring, for 2–3 minutes, or until soft. Add the stock and peas, season with salt and pepper, then bring to the boil. Simmer for 15–20 minutes, or until the peas are very tender.

3 Strain the peas through a sieve and reserve the cooking liquid. Transfer the peas to a food processor or blender and process into a purée, then return the mixture to the pan. Gradually stir in the cooking liquid until you have your desired consistency.

4 Reheat the soup. Stir in the crème fraîche and adjust the seasoning. Serve immediately, with the croûtons and blue cheese sprinkled over.

PEAS PLEASE

Green peas are loaded with antioxidants and anti-inflammatory nutrients, which makes them excellent for good health.

PER SERVING: 343 CALS | 22.6G FAT | 12G SAT FAT | 22.8G CARBS | 7.5G SUGARS | 3.7G SALT | 6G FIBRE | 11.8G PROTEIN

ROAST TOMATO SOUP

If you can't find plum tomatoes, choose whatever variety you have available for this soup; home-grown are best, of course!

SERVES: 4   PREP: 25 MINS   COOK: 1³/4 HOURS

1.3 kg/3 lb plum tomatoes, halved
1 red onion, roughly chopped
6 garlic cloves
4 tbsp virgin olive oil
6 sprigs of fresh thyme, plus extra to garnish
1 litre/1³/4 pints home-made vegetable
stock (see page 16)
juice of ¹/2 lemon
sea salt and pepper

CHEESE CROUTONS
3¹/2 slices of home-made wholemeal bread
(see page 24), cut into cubes
25 g/1 oz Parmesan cheese, finely grated

1 Preheat the oven to 160°C/325°F/Gas Mark 3. Arrange the tomatoes, red onion and garlic on a large baking sheet in a single layer, placing the tomatoes cut-side up. Sprinkle over 2 tablespoons of oil, ¹/2 teaspoon of salt, 1 teaspoon of pepper and the thyme. Roast for 45 minutes, or until soft.

2 To make the cheese croûtons, reduce the oven temperature to 150°C/300°F/Gas Mark 2. Toss the bread with the remaining oil and sprinkle with ¹/2 teaspoon of salt and ¹/2 teaspoon of pepper. Arrange the cubes on a baking sheet in a single layer, then bake for 25 minutes. Sprinkle with the cheese and bake for a further 5 minutes, or until the cheese is beginning to brown.

3 Put the tomato and onion mixture and the stock in a blender or food processor and process to a purée, in batches if necessary.

4 Pour the soup into a large saucepan and bring to the boil over a high heat. Reduce the heat to medium and simmer, stirring occasionally, for 15 minutes. Just before serving, stir in the lemon juice. Serve immediately, with the croûtons and thyme sprinkled over.

ALLIUM ANYONE?

Onion and garlic are both natural antibiotics, which means this soup is a good choice if you're suffering from an infection.

PER SERVING: 315 CALS | 21.9G FAT | 2G SAT FAT | 25.6G CARBS | 7.6G SUGARS | 1.6G SALT | 4.3G FIBRE | 5.8G PROTEIN

BROAD BEAN AND MINT HUMMUS WITH CRUDITES

This summery hummus, made with freshly podded broad beans flavoured with chopped garden herbs and lemon juice, is delicious on warm home-made pittas.

SERVES: 4 PREP: 25 MINS COOK: 10 MINS

350 g/12 oz podded broad beans
2 tbsp virgin olive oil
1 tsp cumin seeds, crushed
3 spring onions, thinly sliced
2 garlic cloves, finely chopped
25 g/1 oz fresh mint, torn into pieces
25 g/1 oz fresh flat-leaf parsley, finely chopped
juice of 1 lemon
60 g/2¼ oz Greek-style natural yogurt
sea salt and pepper

TO SERVE
1 red and 1 yellow pepper, deseeded and cut into strips
4 celery sticks, cut into strips
½ cucumber, halved, deseeded and cut into strips
1 portion of pittas (see page 72), cut into strips (optional)

1 Half-fill the base of a steamer with water, bring to the boil, then put the beans in the steamer top, cover with a lid and steam for 10 minutes, or until tender.

2 Meanwhile, heat the oil in a frying pan over a medium heat. Add the cumin, spring onions and garlic and cook for 2 minutes, or until the onion is softened.

3 Put the beans in a food processor or blender, add the onion mixture, herbs, lemon juice and yogurt and season with a little salt and pepper. Process to a coarse purée, then spoon into a dish set on a large plate.

4 Arrange the vegetable strips around the hummus and serve with the pittas, if using.

WEIGHING BEANS

As a rough guide you will need to buy about 750 g/1 lb 10 oz broad beans in their pods to get about 350 g/12 oz when podded.

PER SERVING: 446 CALS | 13.7G FAT | 2.5G SAT FAT | 67.7G CARBS | 8.4G SUGARS | 2.3G SALT | 15.5G FIBRE | 19.1G PROTEIN

ROOT VEGETABLE CRISPS WITH HERBY YOGURT DIP

Making your own crisps is surprisingly easy and you can be certain there are no added artificial flavourings or preservatives.

SERVES: 4   PREP: 30 MINS
COOK: 16 MINS   COOL: 15 MINS

1 kg/2 lb 4 oz mixed root vegetables, such as carrots, parsnips or sweet potatoes and golden beetroot, very thinly sliced
4 tbsp virgin olive oil
sea salt and pepper

HERBY GARLIC DIP
200 g/7 oz Greek-style natural yogurt
2 garlic cloves, finely chopped
4 tbsp finely chopped fresh herbs, such as flat-leaf parsley, chives, basil and oregano

1 Preheat the oven to 200°C/400°F/Gas Mark 6. To make the herby garlic dip, spoon the yogurt into a jug, then stir in the garlic and herbs and season with salt and pepper. Cover and chill in the refrigerator.

2 Put the vegetables in a large bowl. Slowly drizzle over the oil, gently turning the vegetables as you go, until they are all coated.

3 Arrange the vegetables over three baking sheets in a single layer, then season with salt and pepper. Bake for 8–10 minutes then check – the slices in the corners of the trays will cook more quickly, so transfer any that are crisp and golden to a wire rack. Cook the rest for 2–3 minutes more, then transfer any more cooked crisps to the wire rack. Cook the remaining slices for 2–3 minutes more if needed, then transfer to the wire rack and leave to cool.

4 Arrange the crisps in a bowl and spoon the dip into a smaller bowl, then serve.

SLICING ROOTS

When thinly slicing root vegetables, you should ideally use a mandolin. If you don't have one, a very sharp small knife will do the trick.

PER SERVING: 320 CALS | 16.4G FAT | 3.7G SAT FAT | 37.7G CARBS | 14.7G SUGARS | 1.8G SALT | 8.4G FIBRE | 7.8G PROTEIN

FRUIT, NUT AND SEED TRAIL MIX

This crunchy snack makes a brilliant alternative to commercial crisps for keeping hunger pangs at bay during the day.

MAKES: 400 G/14 OZ (1 SERVING IS 15 G/½ OZ)
PREP: 10 MINS   COOK: 10 MINUTES

200 g/7 oz unblanched almonds
25 g/1 oz pine nuts
25 g/1 oz pumpkin seeds
25 g/1 oz sunflower seeds
25 g/1 oz dried banana chips
55 g/2 oz dates, stoned and roughly chopped
2 tbsp oat bran
½ tsp ground mixed spice
1 small egg white

1 Preheat the oven to 200°C/400°F/Gas Mark 6. Put the almonds, pine nuts, pumpkin and sunflower seeds, banana chips, dates, oat bran and mixed spice in a large bowl and mix well.

2 Lightly beat the egg white with a fork. Add to the nuts, stirring to coat all the ingredients evenly.

3 Spread the mixture out on a large baking sheet in a single layer. Bake for 8–10 minutes, or until crisp and lightly browned.

4 Leave to cool completely. Serve or pack into an airtight container and eat within five days.

ALSO TRY...

For a savoury mix, replace the bananas and dates with 85 g/3 oz cashew nuts, and the mixed spice with 1 teaspoon of mild curry powder and a large pinch of sea salt.

PER SERVING: 75 CALS | 6G FAT | 0.5G SAT FAT | 2.5G CARBS | 1G SUGARS | TRACE SALT | 1G FIBRE | 2.5G PROTEIN

TURKEY GOUJONS WITH RED CABBAGE AND KALE SLAW

Forget deep-fried chicken; this oven-baked, crispy-coated turkey version is quick and easy to make and healthier!

SERVES: 4   PREP: 20 MINS   COOK: 15 MINS

70 g/2^1/$_2$ oz flaxseeds
40 g/1^1/$_2$ oz sesame seeds
2 eggs
450 g/1 lb skinless and boneless turkey breast, thinly sliced
3 tbsp virgin olive oil
sea salt and pepper

RED CABBAGE AND KALE SLAW
115 g/4 oz red cabbage, thinly shredded
25 g/1 oz kale, thinly shredded
1 carrot, coarsely grated
1 dessert apple, cored and coarsely grated
1 tsp caraway seeds
60 g/2^1/$_4$ oz Greek-style natural yogurt

1 Preheat the oven to 220°C/425°F/Gas Mark 7 and put a large baking sheet in it.

2 To make the slaw, put the red cabbage, kale and carrot in a bowl and mix well. Add the apple, caraway seeds and yogurt, season with salt and pepper and mix well. Cover and chill in the refrigerator until needed.

3 Put the flaxseeds in a spice mill or blender and process until roughly chopped. Add the sesame seeds and process for a few seconds. Tip the mixture out onto a plate.

4 Crack the eggs into a shallow dish, season with salt and pepper and beat lightly with a fork.

5 Dip each turkey slice into the eggs, then lift it out with a fork and dip both sides into the seed mixture to coat. Brush the hot baking sheet with a little oil, add the turkey slices in a single layer, then drizzle with a little extra oil.

6 Bake the turkey, turning the slices once and moving them from the corners into the centre of the baking sheet, for 15 minutes, or until golden brown and cooked through. Cut one of the larger turkey goujons in half to check that the meat is no longer pink. Any juices that run out should be clear and piping hot with steam rising. Serve the goujons with the slaw.

MAKE IT LIGHTER

Put a little oil in a small pump-action plastic sprayer and use this to spray a fine oil mist over the turkey before baking.

PER SERVING: 471 CALS | 27G FAT | 4.2G SAT FAT | 21.3G CARBS | 8.6G SUGARS | 1.8G SALT | 9.2G FIBRE | 38.4G PROTEIN

FISH CAKES

These fish cakes can be made and shaped up to a day in advance and stored in the refrigerator, ready to bake 30 minutes before lunch.

SERVES: 4   PREP: 45 MINS
CHILL: 30 MINUTES   COOK: 50 MINUTES

500 g/1 lb 2 oz baking potatoes, cut into chunks
500 g/1 lb 2 oz boneless firm white fish fillets, such as hake, pollack or haddock
25 g/1 oz unsalted butter
finely grated zest and juice of 1 unwaxed lemon
4 tbsp milk
25 g/1 oz fresh flat-leaf parsley, finely chopped
40 g/1 1/2 oz fresh chives, finely snipped
1 egg
4 slices of home-made wholemeal bread (see page 24), processed in a food processor to make crumbs
40 g/1 1/2 oz Parmesan cheese, finely grated
1 tbsp virgin olive oil
sea salt and pepper
85 g/3 oz mixed green salad leaves, to serve
lemon wedges, to serve

OLIVE TARTARE SAUCE

70 g/2 1/2 oz herb-marinated green and black olives, stoned and chopped
150 g/5 1/2 oz natural yogurt

1 Half-fill the base of a steamer with water, bring to the boil, then add the potatoes to the water and cook for 15 minutes. Put the fish in the steamer top in a single layer, cover with a lid and steam for 8–10 minutes, or until it flakes easily when pressed with a knife and the potatoes are tender.

2 Drain the potatoes, add the butter, lemon zest and juice and 2 tablespoons of milk, and mash together. Remove any skin from the fish, flake the flesh into bite-sized pieces, then add it to the mash with 15 g/1/2 oz each of the parsley and chives and a little salt and pepper, and fold everything together carefully.

3 Divide the mixture into eight portions, then shape each into a thick round and leave to cool.

4 Crack the egg into a shallow bowl, add the remaining 2 tablespoons of milk and beat with a fork. Put the breadcrumbs, remaining parsley, 15 g/1/2 oz chives and the Parmesan on a plate and mix together. Coat each fish cake in the egg, then dip it into the crumb mixture to coat completely. Chill in the refrigerator for 30 minutes.

5 Preheat the oven to 200°C/400°F/Gas Mark 6. Brush a large baking sheet with a little oil, add the fish cakes, then drizzle with a little extra oil. Bake for 25–30 minutes, turning over halfway through cooking, until browned and piping hot.

6 To make the olive tartare sauce, put the olives, yogurt, remaining chives and a little salt and pepper in a bowl and mix well. Serve the fish cakes with spoonfuls of the sauce, the green salad leaves and lemon wedges for squeezing over.

BUYING FISH

When buying fish from your local supermarket or fishmonger, look out for the MSC (Marine Stewardship Council) approved logo.

PER SERVING: 400 CALS | 15.9G FAT | 7G SAT FAT | 33.2G CARBS | 5.1G SUGARS | 3.2G SALT | 4.8G FIBRE | 31.3G PROTEIN

STUFFED AUBERGINES

Enjoy this bake with a green salad and baby new potatoes for a sunshine lunch. Quinoa is processed to remove bitter compounds, but its nutrition levels are super high!

SERVES: 4   PREP: 30 MINS   COOK: 50 MINS

2 aubergines
1 tbsp virgin olive oil
1 small onion, finely chopped
2 garlic cloves, finely chopped
140 g/5 oz white quinoa
350 ml/12 fl oz home-made vegetable stock (see page 16)
25 g/1 oz unblanched almonds, thinly sliced and toasted
2 tbsp finely chopped fresh mint, plus a few sprigs to garnish
85 g/3 oz feta cheese, drained and crumbled
sea salt and pepper

1 Preheat the oven to 230°C/450°F/Gas Mark 8. Put the aubergines on a baking sheet and bake for 15 minutes, or until soft. Leave to cool slightly.

2 Cut each aubergine in half lengthways and scoop out the flesh, leaving a 5-mm/1/4-inch-thick border inside the skin so they hold their shape. Chop the flesh.

3 Heat the oil in a large, heavy-based frying pan over a medium-high heat. Add the onion and garlic and cook, stirring occasionally, for 5 minutes, or until soft. Add the quinoa, stock, aubergine flesh, 1 teaspoon of salt and a pinch of pepper. Reduce the heat to medium-low, cover and cook for 15 minutes, or until the quinoa is cooked through. Remove from the heat and stir in the almonds, mint and half the feta.

4 Divide the quinoa mixture equally between the aubergine skins and top with the remaining feta. Bake for 10–15 minutes, or until the feta is bubbling and beginning to brown. Garnish with the mint sprigs and serve.

AUBERGINE FACTS

Aubergines are packed with antioxidants, many B vitamins and minerals such as manganese, copper, iodine and potassium.

PER SERVING: 287 CALS | 14G FAT | 4.2G SAT FAT | 29G CARBS | 9G SUGARS | 2.1G SALT | 9G FIBRE | 12.5G PROTEIN

TAGLIATELLE WITH ROASTED PUMPKIN AND WALNUT PESTO

Roasted pumpkin or butternut squash tastes great with home-made walnut pesto. Make extra pesto and keep it in the refrigerator for up to two days.

SERVES: 4   PREP: 20 MINS   COOK: 25 MINS

1 kg/2 lb 4 oz pumpkin or butternut squash, deseeded, peeled and cut into 2–cm/³/4-inch slices
2 tbsp virgin olive oil
500 g/1 lb 2 oz fresh wholewheat tagliatelle
sea salt flakes and pepper

WALNUT PESTO
85 g/3 oz walnuts, broken into pieces
6 tbsp virgin olive oil
15 g/¹/2 oz fresh basil
25 g/1 oz Parmesan cheese, thinly shaved, plus extra to serve
70 g/2¹/2 oz rocket leaves

1 Preheat the oven to 200° C/400° F/Gas Mark 6. Arrange the pumpkin on a large baking sheet in a single layer. Drizzle with the oil and season with salt and pepper. Roast for 20–25 minutes, or until just tender.

2 Meanwhile, to make the pesto, put the walnuts in a large frying pan and toast for 2–3 minutes, or until just beginning to brown. Transfer to a food processor or blender, pour in the oil and process until coarsely ground. Add the basil, cheese and half the rocket leaves and process again until you have a coarse pesto.

3 Bring a large saucepan of water to the boil, add the tagliatelle and cook for 3–4 minutes, or according to the packet instructions, until al dente.

4 Drain the pasta and pour a little of the cooking water into a jug. Return the pasta to the pan. Cut the pumpkin into cubes and add this to the pasta. Drizzle over the pesto and gently toss together, adding a little of the reserved pasta water if needed to loosen the sauce. Top with the remaining rocket.

5 Spoon into bowls and serve with extra cheese.

MAKE IT LIGHTER

Toss the roasted pumpkin and walnut pesto with crisp salad leaves rather than pasta for a lighter meal.

PER SERVING: 808 CALS | 49.9G FAT | 8.2G SAT FAT | 74.7G CARBS | 4.5G SUGARS | 1.9G SALT | 11.1G FIBRE | 25.5G PROTEIN

ROASTED BEETROOT AND FARRO SALAD

Beetroot is low in fat, full of vitamins and minerals, packed with antioxidants and delicious, especially when it shares a plate with earthy farro and walnuts.

SERVES: 4   PREP: 20 MINS   COOK: 40 MINS

2 raw beetroot (approx 175 g/6 oz), quartered
3 sprigs of fresh thyme
5 tbsp walnut oil
100 g/3½ oz quick-cook farro, rinsed
1 large red pepper, halved lengthways and deseeded
25 g/1 oz walnuts, roughly chopped
85 g/3 oz rocket leaves
thick balsamic vinegar, for drizzling
sea salt and pepper

1 Preheat the oven to 190°C/375°F/Gas Mark 5. Preheat the grill to high. Cut out two squares of foil.

2 Divide the beetroot and thyme between the foil squares. Sprinkle with a little of the oil and season with salt and pepper. Wrap in a loose parcel, sealing the edges, and place on a baking sheet. Roast for 30–40 minutes, or until tender.

3 Meanwhile, put the farro in a saucepan, cover with water and add ½ teaspoon of salt. Bring to the boil, then reduce the heat, cover and simmer for 20 minutes, or according to the pack instructions, until the grains are tender. Drain the farro and tip it into a dish.

4 Meanwhile, put the red pepper halves, cut-side down, on the grill pan and grill for 10 minutes, or until blackened. Cover with a clean tea-towel and leave to stand for 10 minutes. Remove and discard the skin and roughly chop the flesh.

5 Divide the cooked farro between four plates. Slice the beetroot quarters in half, arrange on top of the farro and toss. Scatter over the red pepper, walnuts and rocket.

6 Drizzle with the remaining oil and some balsamic vinegar. Serve immediately.

ALSO TRY...

This salad works equally well with barley instead of farro. The barley will need boiling for 35 minutes.

PER SERVING: 315 CALS | 21.9G FAT | 2G SAT FAT | 25.6G CARBS | 7.6G SUGARS | 1.6G SALT | 4.3G FIBRE | 5.8G PROTEIN

WHOLEWHEAT SPINACH, PEA AND FETA TART

Baked and unfilled tart cases freeze well, so why not make two, then fill and enjoy one now and wrap and freeze the second for another time?

SERVES: 6   PREP: 30 MINS
CHILL: 30 MINS   COOK: 1 HOUR 10 MINS   COOL: 20 MINS

15 g/1/2 oz unsalted butter
3 spring onions, thinly sliced
200 g/7 oz baby spinach
100 g/31/2 oz podded peas
3 eggs
250 ml/9 fl oz milk
100 g/31/2 oz feta cheese, drained and finely crumbled
115 g/4 oz cherry tomatoes
sea salt and pepper

PASTRY
115 g/4 oz unsalted butter, cut into cubes
225 g/8 oz wholemeal plain flour, plus extra to dust
2 eggs, beaten

PASTRY TIPS

Wholemeal flour adds a wonderful nuttiness to pastry, but can be difficult to handle. If it breaks when you line the tart tin, just press the cracks together or patch with some of the trimmings and stick in place with any remaining egg or a little water.

1 To make the pastry, put the butter and flour in a mixing bowl and season with salt and pepper. Rub the butter into the flour until it resembles fine crumbs. Gradually mix in enough egg to make a soft but not sticky dough.

2 Lightly dust a work surface with wholemeal flour. Knead the pastry gently, then roll it out on the work surface to a little larger than a 25-cm/10-inch loose-bottomed flan tin. Lift the pastry over the rolling pin, ease it into the tin and press it into the sides. Trim the pastry so that it stands a little above the top of the tin to allow for shrinkage, then prick the base with a fork.

3 Cover the tart case with clingfilm and chill in the refrigerator for 15–30 minutes. Meanwhile, preheat the oven to 190°C/375°F/Gas Mark 5.

4 To make the filling, melt the butter in a frying pan over a medium heat. Add the spring onions and cook for 2–3 minutes, or until softened. Add the spinach, turn the heat to high, and cook, stirring, until wilted. Set aside to cool.

5 Cook the peas in a small saucepan of boiling water for 2 minutes. Drain, then plunge into iced water and drain again. Crack the eggs into a jug, add the milk, season with salt and pepper and beat with a fork.

6 Line the tart case with a large sheet of baking paper, add baking beans and place on a baking sheet. Bake for 10 minutes, then remove the paper and beans and bake for 5 minutes more, or until the base of the tart is crisp and dry.

7 Drain any cooking juices from the spring onions and spinach into the eggs. Put the onion mixture in the tart case, add the peas, then sprinkle over the cheese. Fork the eggs and milk together once more, then pour into the tart case and dot the tomatoes over the top. Bake for 40–50 minutes, or until set and golden. Leave to cool for 20 minutes, then serve.

PER SERVING: 458 CALS | 29.4G FAT | 16.9G SAT FAT | 34.9G CARBS | 4.8G SUGARS | 2.1G SALT | 6G FIBRE | 16.8G PROTEIN

ROASTED MEDITERRANEAN VEGETABLE PIZZAS

Making your own pizzas might seem like a lot of work, but they are actually very easy to put together and a great way to encourage children to cook.

SERVES: 4   PREP: 50 MINS
RISE: 1 HOUR   COOK: 30 MINS

500 g/1 lb 2 oz plum tomatoes, halved
1 red onion, cut into 8 wedges
1 aubergine, halved and sliced
1 red and 1 orange pepper, quartered and deseeded
2 small courgettes, sliced
3 tbsp virgin olive oil, plus extra to serve
15 g/¹⁄₂ oz basil leaves, plus extra to garnish
2 tsp aged balsamic vinegar
175 g/6 oz goat's cheese, crumbled
sea salt flakes and coarsely ground black pepper

PIZZA BASES
250 g/9 oz wholemeal plain flour, plus extra to dust
¹⁄₂ tsp sea salt
1 tsp dark muscovado sugar
1 tsp easy-blend dried yeast
1 tbsp virgin olive oil
150–175 ml/5–6 fl oz warm water

1 Preheat the oven to 220°C/425°F/Gas Mark 7. To make the pizza bases, put the flour, salt, sugar and yeast in a mixing bowl and stir. Add the oil, then gradually mix in enough warm water to make a soft but not sticky dough.

2 Lightly dust a work surface with flour. Knead the dough on the surface for 5 minutes, until smooth and elastic. Return it to the bowl, cover with a clean tea-towel and put it in a warm place for 45 minutes, or until doubled in size.

3 Arrange the tomatoes and red onion on a baking sheet in a single layer. Arrange the aubergine and peppers, cut-side down, on a second baking sheet in a single layer. Arrange the courgettes on a third baking sheet in a single layer. Drizzle with a little oil and sprinkle with salt and pepper. Roast for 15 minutes, then take out the courgettes. Roast the other two trays for 5 minutes more. Wrap the peppers in foil and leave to cool, then cut into slices.

4 Remove and discard the tomato skins, if liked, then chop the tomatoes, onion and basil and mix with the vinegar.

5 Lightly flour two baking sheets. Knead the dough, cut it into two pieces and roll out each piece into an oval 30 cm/ 12 inches long by 15 cm/6 inches wide. Transfer them to the baking sheets, spoon over the tomato mixture, then top with the roasted vegetables. Leave to rise for 15 minutes.

6 Sprinkle the goat's cheese over the pizzas, then bake for 10 minutes, or until the bases are cooked and the cheese has melted. Sprinkle with a little extra oil and basil. Cut each pizza into wedges and serve immediately.

FABULOUS FRESH YEAST

Easy-blend dried yeast makes a great store-cupboard standby, but if you would rather use fresh yeast, try to buy it from your local baker. Crumble 2 teaspoons of fresh yeast and mix it with the sugar, then blend with half the warm water. Set aside for 15 minutes, or until the liquid begins to froth, then mix into the flour with the remaining ingredients. Keep any leftover yeast in paper in an airtight container in the refrigerator for no more than three days.

PER SERVING: 595 CALS | 30.3G FAT | 11.2G SAT FAT | 66.1G CARBS | 13.2G SUGARS | 2.8G SALT | 14.3G FIBRE | 21.6G PROTEIN

BEETROOT FALAFEL WITH PITTAS

Traditionally deep fried, these ruby-coloured falafel are flavoured with cumin and sumac then roasted. Serve in home-made pittas with spoonfuls of tzatziki and lettuce.

SERVES: 4   PREP: 1 HOUR
RISE: 55 MINS   COOK: 35 MINS

little wholemeal plain flour, to dust
1 quantity kneaded and risen pizza base dough (see page 70) made with 1 tsp roughly crushed cumin seeds added with the yeast
2 x 400 g cans of chickpeas in water, drained
1 red onion, finely chopped
2 garlic cloves, thinly sliced
1 tsp cumin seeds, roughly crushed
1 tsp sumac seeds
1 tsp baking powder
2 raw beetroot (approx 175 g/6 oz), coarsely grated
3 tbsp virgin olive oil, to brush
sea salt and pepper
lettuce leaves, shredded, to serve

TZATZIKI
1/2 cucumber, halved, deseeded and finely chopped
150 g/5¹/2 oz natural yogurt
2 tbsp finely chopped fresh mint

1 Preheat the oven to 220°C/425°F/Gas Mark 7. To make the pittas, lightly dust a work surface with flour. Knead the dough gently, then cut it into four pieces and roll out each piece on the work surface into an oval about the size of your hand. Leave to rise for 10 minutes.

2 Lightly flour two baking sheets, then put them in the oven for 5 minutes. Add the breads to the hot baking sheets and bake for 5–10 minutes, or until puffed and lightly browned. Wrap them in a clean tea–towel to keep them soft.

3 Meanwhile, put the chickpeas in a food processor or blender, in small batches, and process into a coarse paste, scraping down the sides of the goblet several times with a spatula. Tip them into a bowl. Add the onion, garlic, cumin, sumac, baking powder and beetroot, season well with salt and pepper, then mix together with a fork.

4 Spoon the mixture into 20 mounds on a chopping board, then squeeze them into balls. Brush a large roasting tin with a little oil, then put it in the oven for 5 minutes. Add the falafel and brush generously with more oil. Roast for 20–25 minutes, turning once or twice, until browned and the chickpeas and beetroot are cooked through; break one open and taste to check.

5 Meanwhile, to make the tzatziki, put the cucumber, yogurt and mint in a bowl, season with salt and pepper and mix well.

6 To serve, split the warm pittas open, spoon in the shredded lettuce, tzatziki and falafel and serve.

FREEZING PITTAS

Make a double quantity of pittas and freeze half the cooked breads in a sealed plastic bag. Defrost at room temperature for 1 hour, then warm in a frying pan for 2 minutes on each side.

PER SERVING: 638 CALS | 21.8G FAT | 3.5G SAT FAT | 93.4G CARBS | 14.1G SUGARS | 2.5G SALT | 19.9G FIBRE | 23.3G PROTEIN

MAINS

Spicy beef burgers with guacamole and wedges	76
Yam and beef stew with wholegrain couscous	79
Roast pork with rosemary potatoes	81
Spiced turkey stew with wholegrain couscous	82
Chicken with pomegranate and beetroot tabbouleh	84
Cheddar and apple-stuffed chicken breasts	86
Seared wild salmon with garden greens	88
Butter-fried sole	90
Parsnip and tomato bake	92
Quinoa with roasted vegetables	94
Vegetable cocido	96
Squash, kale and farro stew	99

SPICY BEEF BURGERS WITH GUACAMOLE AND WEDGES

A good beef burger is hard to beat, and if you make your own you'll know what is in it and where the meat has come from. Mince the steak in a food processor or hand mincer.

SERVES: 4   PREP: 1 HOUR
RISE: 1½ HOURS   COOK: 1 HOUR

500 g/1 lb 2 oz rump steak, visible fat removed, diced
½ tsp chilli powder
2 tsp cumin seeds, roughly crushed
1 tbsp fresh thyme leaves
700 g/1 lb 9 oz baking potatoes, unpeeled, scrubbed and cut into wedges
3 tbsp virgin olive oil
1 tsp paprika
sea salt and pepper

GUACAMOLE
1 large avocado, stoned and peeled
juice of 1 lime
2 spring onions, finely chopped

TO SERVE
4 spelt breakfast rolls (see page 38, but shape 10 rolls instead of 16, leave to rise for 45 minutes instead of overnight and bake for 15–18 minutes), halved
1 romaine lettuce heart, shredded
handful of rocket leaves
2 large tomatoes, sliced

1 Preheat the oven to 200°C/400°F/Gas Mark 6. With the motor running on a food processor, drop in a few pieces of steak at a time, until it has all been roughly chopped. Alternatively, press the pieces through a mincer on the coarse setting.

2 Put the chilli powder, half the cumin seeds, half the thyme and a little salt and pepper in a bowl and mix well. Rub this into the steak, then shape the mixture into four burgers. Cover and chill in the refrigerator for 15 minutes.

3 Meanwhile, bring a saucepan of water to the boil, add the wedges and cook for 4–5 minutes, or until almost tender. Drain well and tip into a roasting tin. Drizzle the wedges with 2 tablespoons of oil, then turn them several times until they are well coated. Sprinkle with the paprika, remaining cumin and thyme and a little salt and pepper. Bake, turning once, for 25–30 minutes, or until golden brown.

4 For the guacamole, put the avocado in a shallow bowl and mash with a fork. Add the lime juice and spring onions, season with a little salt and pepper and mix well.

5 Preheat the grill to medium–high. Brush the burgers with a little of the remaining oil, then cook, turning halfway through, for 8–10 minutes, or a little less for those who like their burgers pink in the middle. Leave to stand for a few minutes. Meanwhile, toast the rolls, then top the bases with lettuce, rocket and tomatoes, the hot burgers, and a spoonful of guacamole and the roll lids. Serve with the wedges.

AVOCADO TIP

Avocado flesh quickly goes brown, even when mixed with lime juice, so don't be tempted to peel and mash the flesh for the guacamole until you are ready to cook the burgers.

PER SERVING: 695 CALS | 28.9G FAT | 5.8G SAT FAT | 63.4G CARBS | 9.9G SUGARS | 1.4G SALT | 13.8G FIBRE | 49.1G PROTEIN

YAM AND BEEF STEW WITH WHOLEGRAIN COUSCOUS

Your kitchen will be filled with delicious smells as this warming and nutritious dish slowly simmers in your oven, leaving you to get on with something else.

SERVES: 4   PREP: 30 MINS
CHILL: OVERNIGHT   COOK: 1½ HOURS

800 g/1 lb 12 oz stewing beef, cut into 2.5–cm/1–inch cubes
2 onions, roughly chopped
200 g/7 oz yams, cut into cubes
200 g/7 oz baby new potatoes, unpeeled, scrubbed and halved
400 g/14 oz canned chickpeas in water, drained and rinsed
400 g/14 oz canned chopped tomatoes
200 ml/7 fl oz water
sea salt and pepper

MARINADE
2 tbsp virgin olive oil
2 tbsp finely chopped fresh coriander
2 cinnamon sticks
1 tbsp runny honey
1 tsp paprika
1 tsp ground cumin
1 tsp harissa paste

COUSCOUS
200 g/7 oz wholegrain couscous
1 tbsp roughly chopped fresh flat–leaf parsley
6 spring onions, thinly sliced
juice of 1 lemon
2 tbsp virgin olive oil

1 Put the beef in a large bowl. Add the marinade ingredients and 1 teaspoon of salt and stir well. Cover and chill in the refrigerator for 6 hours or overnight.

2 Preheat the oven to 190°C/375°F/Gas Mark 5. Transfer the meat and marinade to a casserole dish and add the onions, yams, potatoes and chickpeas. Pour over the tomatoes and water and stir well. Bake for 1 hour.

3 Stir well and check the seasoning. If most of the liquid has been absorbed, add enough water to create a generous sauce. Bake for a further 30 minutes, or until the meat is cooked and tender.

4 Meanwhile, half–fill a saucepan with water and bring to the boil. Add the couscous and cook according to the packet instructions, or until just tender. Tip into a sieve and drain well. Transfer to a bowl, stir in the parsley and spring onions, then drizzle over the lemon juice and oil.

5 Remove the cinnamon sticks from the stew and serve with the couscous.

PER SERVING: 836 CALS | 29.2G FAT | 7.3G SAT FAT | 88G CARBS | 12.6G SUGARS | 2.9G SALT | 13.3G FIBRE | 57.4G PROTEIN

cook for 4–5 minutes. Drain well and tip into a roasting tin. Drizzle with the remaining oil, then turn the potatoes several times until they are well coated. Roast, turning once, for 40 minutes, or until golden brown.

4 Transfer the pork and potatoes to a serving platter and scatter the potatoes with a little salt. Serve immediately with the pork.

ROAST POTATOES

Choose a floury variety, such as Maris Piper, King Edward or Desiree, for roasting as these crisp up better.

PER SERVING: 674 CALS | 39.7G FAT | 11G SAT FAT | 26G CARBS | 1.9G SUGARS | 2.3G SALT | 4G FIBRE | 51G PROTEIN

SPICED TURKEY STEW WITH WHOLEGRAIN GIANT COUSCOUS

Capture the flavours of Middle Eastern cooking with this easy, lightly spiced stove-top turkey stew.

SERVES: 4   PREP: 20 MINS   COOK: 25 MINS

1 tbsp virgin olive oil
500 g/1 lb 2 oz skinless and boneless turkey breast, cut into 1.5–cm/³/4–inch pieces
1 onion, roughly chopped
2 garlic cloves, finely chopped
1 red and 1 orange pepper, deseeded and roughly chopped
500 g/1 lb 2 oz tomatoes, roughly chopped
1 tsp cumin seeds, roughly crushed
1 tsp paprika
finely grated zest and juice of 1 unwaxed lemon
sea salt and pepper

TO SERVE

200 g/7 oz wholegrain giant couscous
2 tbsp roughly chopped fresh flat-leaf parsley
2 tbsp roughly chopped fresh coriander

1 Heat the oil in a large frying pan over a medium heat. Add the turkey, a few pieces at a time, then add the onion. Fry, stirring, for 5 minutes, or until the turkey is golden.

2 Add the garlic, red and orange peppers and tomatoes, then stir in the cumin seeds and paprika. Add the lemon juice and season with salt and pepper. Stir well, then cover and cook, stirring from time to time, for 20 minutes, or until the tomatoes have formed a thick sauce and the turkey is cooked through and the juices run clear with no sign of pink when a piece is cut in half.

3 Meanwhile, half-fill a saucepan with water and bring to the boil. Add the couscous and cook according to the packet instructions, or until just tender. Tip into a sieve and drain well.

4 Spoon the couscous onto plates and top with the turkey stew. Mix the parsley and coriander with the lemon zest, then sprinkle over the stew and serve.

GOOD TURKEY

Turkey makes a great low-fat, quick-cook supper, especially without the skin.

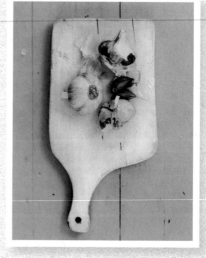

PER SERVING: 399 CALS | 6.6G FAT | 1.3G SAT FAT | 36G CARBS | 8.1G SUGARS | 0.9G SALT | 7.2G FIBRE | 37.5G PROTEIN

CHICKEN WITH POMEGRANATE AND BEETROOT TABBOULEH

This version of tabbouleh is made with wholegrain wheatberries. High in fibre, it is a great alternative to rice or pasta.

SERVES: 4 PREP: 25 MINS COOK: 25 MINS

225 g/8 oz wheatberries
4 raw beetroot (approx 350 g/12 oz), cut into cubes
500 g/1 lb 2 oz skinless and boneless chicken breasts, thinly sliced
1 small red onion, thinly sliced
200 g/7 oz cherry tomatoes, halved
seeds of 1 small pomegranate
2 tbsp roughly chopped fresh mint
70 g/2¹/2 oz baby spinach
sea salt and pepper

DRESSING
juice of 1 lemon
4 tbsp virgin olive oil
2 garlic cloves, finely chopped
1 tsp light muscovado sugar

1 Half-fill the base of a steamer with water, bring to the boil, then add the wheatberries to the water. Put the beetroot in the steamer top, cover with a lid and steam for 20–25 minutes, or until the wheatberries and beetroot are cooked. Drain the wheatberries.

2 Meanwhile, to make the dressing, put the lemon juice, oil, garlic and sugar in a jam jar, season with salt and pepper, then screw on the lid and shake well.

3 Put the chicken in a bowl, add half the dressing and toss well. Preheat a griddle pan over a medium-high heat. Add the chicken and cook, turning once or twice, for 8–10 minutes, or until golden and cooked through. Cut one of the larger slices of chicken in half to check that the meat is no longer pink. Any juices that run out should be clear and piping hot with steam rising.

4 Put the red onion, tomatoes and pomegranate seeds in a large shallow bowl. Add the wheatberries, beetroot and mint. Divide the spinach between four plates, spoon the wheatberry mixture over them, then arrange the chicken on top. Serve with the remaining dressing in a small jug.

LOVE LEFTOVERS

Leftovers can be packed into a plastic container and stored in the refrigerator, but keep the dressing separate so the salad doesn't go limp.

PER SERVING: 545 CALS | 17.2G FAT | 2G SAT FAT | 62.2G CARBS | 15G SUGARS | 1.1G SALT | 12.3G FIBRE | 39.4G PROTEIN

CHEDDAR AND APPLE-STUFFED CHICKEN BREASTS

A new and tasty spin on chicken Kiev, this simple and delicious dish is sure to be a hit with the family!

SERVES: 4 PREP: 30 MINS COOK: 35 MINS

4 thick skinless and boneless chicken breasts
1 tbsp virgin olive oil, plus extra to grease
1 small onion, finely chopped
1 celery stick, finely chopped
1/4 tsp dried sage
1 dessert apple, cored and diced
85 g/3 oz Cheddar cheese, coarsely grated
2 tbsp finely chopped fresh flat-leaf parsley
6 slices of Parma ham, visible fat removed
sea salt and pepper
150 g/5 1/2 oz Tenderstem broccoli, to serve
150 g/5 1/2 oz podded peas, to serve

AMAZING APPLES

Apples are rich in the disease-fighting compounds, antioxidants. They are also rich in beta-carotene and vitamin C, and contain B-complex vitamins such as riboflavin and thiamin.

1 Preheat the oven to 190°C/375°F/Gas Mark 5. Lightly oil a small roasting tin.

2 Put a chicken breast on a chopping board, rounded side up. Use a small, sharp knife to cut a pocket along the length of the chicken breast, cutting as deep as you can without cutting through to the other side or the ends. Repeat with the remaining breasts, then cover and transfer to the refrigerator.

3 To make the stuffing, heat 2 teaspoons of oil in a frying pan over a medium heat. Add the onion, celery and sage and fry, stirring, for 3–5 minutes, or until soft. Stir in the apple and fry for 2 minutes, or until soft but not falling apart. Stir in the cheese and parsley and season with salt and pepper.

4 Divide the stuffing between the fillet pockets. Wrap one and a half slices of ham around each breast, then rub the tops with the remaining oil.

5 Transfer the chicken to the prepared tin and roast for 20–25 minutes, or until the chicken is cooked through and the juices are piping hot with steam rising and run clear with no sign of pink when a skewer is inserted into the thickest part of the meat.

6 Cover with foil and leave to stand for 3–5 minutes. Bring a saucepan of water to the boil, add the broccoli and peas and cook for 3–4 minutes, then drain well. Serve the chicken with the green vegetables.

PER SERVING: 329 CALS | 17G FAT | 6.8G SAT FAT | 8G CARBS | 5.2G SUGARS | 2.1G SALT | 1.5G FIBRE | 35G PROTEIN

SEARED WILD SALMON WITH GARDEN GREENS

Quick and easy to prepare, this light and summery supper makes the best of the early beans and asparagus.

SERVES: 4 PREP: 20 MINS COOK: 15 MINS

500 g/1 lb 2 oz baby new potatoes, unpeeled, scrubbed and any larger ones halved
1 tbsp virgin olive oil
finely grated zest and juice of 1 unwaxed lemon
1 tsp set honey
1 tsp wholegrain mustard
4 x 150 g/5½ oz wild salmon steaks
250 g/9 oz runner beans, cut into thin slices
250 g/9 oz asparagus
175 g/6 oz baby peas in pods or sugar snap peas
1 fennel bulb, thinly sliced, green feathery tops torn into pieces
6 tbsp crème fraîche
sea salt and pepper

1 Half-fill the base of a steamer with water, bring to the boil, then add the potatoes to the water and cook for 15 minutes.

2 Preheat the grill to medium-high and line the grill pan with foil. Mix the oil, lemon zest and juice, honey and mustard together in a jug, then stir in a little salt and pepper. Arrange the salmon on the grill pan, spoon over the lemon mixture and grill, turning once, for 8–10 minutes, or until browned and the fish flakes easily when pressed with a knife.

3 Put the beans in the steamer, set over the potatoes, cover with a lid and steam for the last 6 minutes. Add the asparagus and sugar snap peas 3 minutes before the end of the cooking time. Add the sliced fennel 1 minute before the end of the cooking time.

4 Drain the potatoes, season with salt and pepper and roughly crush with a fork. Spoon into the centre of four plates. Mix the green vegetables with the crème fraîche and fennel tops, then spoon over the potatoes. Remove the skin from the salmon, then lay it on top of the vegetables and spoon over the lemony pan juices. Serve immediately.

BUYING SALMON

Salmon farming has quadrupled in the last 20 years, so check the label carefully to ensure it is wild, and don't be afraid to ask the assistant where it was caught.

PER SERVING: 528 CALS | 27.7G FAT | 7.2G SAT FAT | 32.9G CARBS | 9.1G SUGARS | 1.1G SALT | 7.9G FIBRE | 37.3G PROTEIN

BUTTER-FRIED SOLE

Look for sustainable fish caught the day you plan to eat it – the flavour will be so much better! Frozen fish is also recommended as it's often caught and frozen on the same day.

SERVES: 2   PREP: 20 MINS   COOK: 12 MINS

100 ml/3½ fl oz milk
60 g/2¼ oz brown rice flour
4 x 175 g/6 oz sole fillets, skinned
85 g/3 oz unsalted butter
juice of ½ lemon, plus 1 lemon, cut into wedges, to serve
sea salt and pepper
2 tbsp roughly chopped fresh flat-leaf parsley, to garnish
250 g/9 oz asparagus, to serve

BUYING ASPARAGUS

To check for freshness, bend the base of the asparagus – you should only be able to bend the very end of it.

1 Pour the milk into a shallow bowl at least as large as each fillet and put the flour on a plate. Season each fillet on both sides with salt and pepper.

2 Bring a saucepan of water to the boil, add the asparagus and cook for 3–5 minutes, then drain well and keep warm.

3 Working with one sole fillet at a time, pull it very quickly through the milk, then dip it in the flour, turn once to coat all over and shake off any excess flour. Transfer it to a plate and continue until all the fillets are prepared.

4 Melt half the butter in a frying pan large enough to hold the fillets in a single layer, over a medium–high heat. Add the fillets, skinned-side down, and fry for 2 minutes.

5 Turn over the fillets and fry for 2–3 minutes, or until the flesh flakes easily. Transfer to two plates, skinned-side up, and set aside.

6 Reduce the heat to medium and melt the remaining butter in the pan. When it stops foaming, add the lemon juice and stir, scraping the sediment from the base of the pan. Spoon the butter mixture over the fish and garnish with parsley. Serve with the asparagus and lemon wedges.

PER SERVING: 753 CALS | 44.1G FAT | 24.5G SAT FAT | 39G CARBS | 6.2G SUGARS | 4.9G SALT | 7.7G FIBRE | 52.7G PROTEIN

PARSNIP AND TOMATO BAKE

Serve this bake with salad and home-made wholemeal bread (see page 24) as a vegetarian supper, or as a side dish with roast meat.

SERVES: 4   PREP: 30 MINS   COOK: 50 MINS

3 tbsp virgin olive oil
600 g/1 lb 5 oz parsnips, thinly sliced lengthways
1 tsp fresh thyme leaves
300 ml/10 fl oz double cream
600 g/1 lb 5 oz tomatoes, thinly sliced
1 tsp dried oregano
150 g/5^{1}/$_2$ oz Cheddar cheese, grated
sea salt and pepper

1 Preheat the oven to 180°C/350°F/Gas Mark 4. Heat the oil in a frying pan over a medium heat. Add the parsnips and thyme and season with salt and pepper. Cook, stirring often, for 6–8 minutes, or until softened. Do this in batches if necessary.

2 Spread half the parsnips over the base of a gratin dish. Pour over half the cream, then arrange half the tomatoes in an even layer on top. Season with salt and pepper and scatter over half the oregano and half the cheese. Top with the remaining parsnips and tomatoes. Sprinkle with remaining oregano, season with salt and pepper and pour over the remaining cream. Scatter over the remaining cheese.

3 Cover with foil and bake for 40 minutes, or until the parsnips are tender. Remove the foil and return to the oven for 5–10 minutes, or until the top is golden and bubbling. Serve immediately.

ALSO TRY...

Use Parmesan cheese instead of Cheddar, or mozzarella for a pizza-style stringy texture.

PER SERVING: 639 CALS | 51G FAT | 26.7G SAT FAT | 35.4G CARBS | 11.4G SUGARS | 1.4G SALT | 9.1G FIBRE | 13.9G PROTEIN

QUINOA WITH ROASTED VEGETABLES

Quinoa is an excellent source of protein, especially for vegetarians, as it contains all nine essential amino acids, which is unsusal for a plant.

SERVES: 2 PREP: 20 MINS COOK: 30 MINS

1 red and 1 yellow pepper, deseeded and roughly chopped
1 large courgette, roughly chopped
1 small fennel bulb, trimmed and cut into thin wedges
1 tbsp virgin olive oil
2 tsp finely chopped fresh rosemary leaves
1 tsp finely chopped fresh thyme leaves
100 g/3½ oz white quinoa, rinsed
350 ml/12 fl oz home-made vegetable stock (see page 16)
2 garlic cloves, crushed
3 tbsp finely chopped fresh flat-leaf parsley
40 g/1½ oz pine nuts, toasted
sea salt and pepper

1 Preheat the oven to 220°C/425°F/Gas Mark 7. Arrange the peppers, courgette and fennel in a large roasting tin in a single layer. Drizzle the oil over the vegetables and scatter on the rosemary and thyme. Season with salt and pepper and mix well. Roast for 25–30 minutes, or until tender and lightly charred.

2 Meanwhile, put the quinoa in a saucepan. Add the stock and garlic, bring to the boil, then cover and simmer over a very low heat for 10 minutes. Remove from the heat, but leave the pan covered for 7 minutes more to allow the grains to swell. Fluff up with a fork.

3 Tip the quinoa into the roasting tin. Add the parsley and pine nuts and toss well. Serve warm or cold.

ALSO TRY...

Use long-grain brown rice instead of quinoa; brown rice takes around 30–45 minutes to cook.

PER SERVING: 471 CALS | 25.3G FAT | 3.1G SAT FAT | 50.6G CARBS | 10.2G SUGARS | 3.2G SALT | 9.7G FIBRE | 13.3G PROTEIN

VEGETABLE COCIDO

Quick and easy to make, this comforting Spanish-inspired stew is flavoured with smoked paprika for a lovely, deep spicy flavour.

SERVES: 4   PREP: 20 MINS   COOK: 50 MINS

2 tbsp virgin olive oil
1 onion, roughly chopped
1 aubergine, roughly chopped
1/2 tsp smoked hot paprika
2 garlic cloves, finely chopped
1 large red pepper, deseeded and roughly chopped
250 g/9 oz baby new potatoes, unpeeled and any larger ones halved
450 g/1 lb plum tomatoes, skinned and roughly chopped
410 g/14 1/2 oz canned haricot beans in water, drained
150 ml/5 fl oz home-made vegetable stock (see page 16)
2 sprigs of fresh rosemary
2 courgettes, roughly chopped
sea salt and pepper

1 Heat 1 tablespoon of oil in a saucepan over a medium heat. Add the onion and fry for 5 minutes, or until softened. Add another tablespoon of oil, then add the aubergine, and fry, stirring, for 5 minutes, or until just beginning to soften and brown.

2 Stir in the smoked paprika and garlic, then the red pepper, potatoes and tomatoes. Add the haricot beans, stock and rosemary, then season with salt and pepper. Bring to the boil, cover, turn the heat down to medium–low and simmer for 30 minutes, stirring from time to time.

3 Stir the courgettes into the stew, then cook, uncovered, for 10 minutes, or until all the vegetables are tender and the sauce has reduced slightly.

4 Ladle the stew into shallow bowls, discard the rosemary sprigs and serve.

SMOKED PAPRIKA

If you haven't used smoked hot paprika before, check before buying as it comes in two heat strengths: hot with the strength of chilli powder or mild. Either one adds a great smoky flavour to this stew.

PER SERVING: 525 CALS | 26.1G FAT | 12.6G SAT FAT | 62.3G CARBS | 14.8G SUGARS | 1.8G SALT | 18.5G FIBRE | 14.6G PROTEIN

SQUASH, KALE AND FARRO STEW

This one-pot is super-easy to make and jam-packed with nutrient-rich vegetables, grains and pulses.

SERVES: 6 PREP: 30 MINS COOK: 55 MINS

2 tbsp virgin olive oil
1 onion, finely chopped
2 tsp dried oregano
2 garlic cloves, thinly sliced
1 x 1.25 kg/2 lb 12 oz dense-fleshed squash,
such as Kabocha or Crown Prince, peeled, deseeded
and flesh cut into large cubes
400 g/14 oz canned chopped tomatoes
700 ml/1¼ pints home-made vegetable
stock (see page 16)
125 g/4½ oz quick-cook farro, rinsed
250 g/9 oz kale, cut into ribbons
400 g/14 oz canned chickpeas in water,
drained and rinsed
25 g/1 oz fresh coriander, roughly chopped
juice of 1 lime
sea salt and pepper

1 Heat the oil in a flameproof casserole dish or heavy-based saucepan over a medium heat. Add the onion and fry for 5 minutes, or until soft. Add the oregano and garlic and fry for 2 minutes.

2 Add the squash and cook, covered, for 10 minutes. Add the tomatoes, stock and farro, cover and bring to the boil. Reduce the heat to medium-low and gently simmer for 20 minutes, stirring occasionally.

3 Add the kale and chickpeas and cook for a further 15 minutes, or until all the vegetables and farro are tender.

4 Season with salt and pepper, and stir in the coriander and lime juice, just before serving.

QUICK-COOK FARRO

Use quick-cook farro (farro dicocco) so you can add it straight to the casserole without lengthy soaking or pre-cooking. It may seem as if there is too much stock, but once you add the farro most of it will be absorbed.

PER SERVING: 302 CALS | 7.7G FAT | 1.4G SAT FAT | 52.4G CARBS | 9.1G SUGARS | 2.4G SALT | 8.9G FIBRE | 10.4G PROTEIN

DESSERTS AND BAKING

CELEBRATION CHOCOLATE CAKE

No-one would guess from the appearance of this indulgent-looking cake that it is made with cooked beetroot for natural sweetness and wholemeal and brown rice flours.

SERVES 8　PREP: 40 MINS
COOK: 1 HOUR 20 MINS　COOL: 15 MINS

2 raw beetroot (approx 200 g/7 oz), cut into cubes
150 g/5¹/2 oz plain chocolate with 70% cocoa, broken into pieces
25 g/1 oz unsweetened cocoa powder
2 tsp baking powder
115 g/4 oz wholemeal plain flour
55 g/2 oz brown rice flour
200 g/7 oz unsalted butter, softened and diced, plus extra to grease
215 g/7¹/2 oz light muscovado sugar
4 eggs
2 tbsp milk
300 ml/10 fl oz double cream

1 Preheat the oven to 160°C/325°F/Gas Mark 3. Lightly butter a 20-cm/8-inch diameter round non-stick springform cake tin and line the base with a circle of baking paper.

2 Half-fill the base of a steamer with water, bring to the boil, then put the beetroot in the steamer top, cover with a lid and steam for 15 minutes, or until tender. Transfer it to a food processor and add 4 tablespoons of water from the base of the steamer. Purée until smooth, then leave to cool.

3 Put 115 g/4 oz of the chocolate in a heatproof bowl set over a saucepan of gently simmering water, ensuring the bowl doesn't touch the water. Leave for 5 minutes, or until the chocolate has melted.

4 Sift the cocoa into a second bowl, then stir in the baking powder and wholemeal and rice flours.

5 Cream the butter and 200 g/7 oz sugar together in a large bowl. Beat in the eggs, one by one, adding spoonfuls of the flour mixture between each egg and beating well after each addition. Stir in the remaining flour mixture, the puréed beetroot and melted chocolate, and beat until smooth, then mix in enough of the milk to make a soft dropping consistency.

6 Spoon the mixture into the prepared tin and spread it into an even layer. Bake for 1 hour, or until well risen, the top is slightly cracked and a skewer comes out cleanly when inserted into the centre of the cake. Leave to cool for 15 minutes, then remove from the tin, peel off the baking paper and transfer the cake to a wire rack.

7 To finish, melt the remaining chocolate in a heatproof bowl set over a saucepan of gently simmering water, ensuring the bowl doesn't touch the water. Put the cream in a bowl, add the remaining sugar and whisk until soft swirls form. Cut the cake in half and put the bottom half on a serving plate. Spoon one-third of the cream mixture onto the base of the cake, add the top half of the cake, then spoon the remaining cream on the top. Drizzle with the melted chocolate. Cut into eight wedges to serve.

PLAIN CHOCOLATE

Studies show that eating a little plain chocolate every day can help lower your blood pressure.

PER SERVING: 662 CALS | 46.2G FAT | 27.5G SAT FAT | 57G CARBS | 33.7G SUGARS | 1G SALT | 5.7G FIBRE | 9.5G PROTEIN

RAW CHOCOLATE ICE CREAM

*No-one will guess that this super-simple ice cream actually contains no chocolate,
but instead is packed with healthy bananas and cocoa powder!*

SERVES: 4   PREP: 10 MINS   FREEZE: 3 HOURS

3 (300 g/10½ oz) bananas, peeled
3 tbsp unsweetened cocoa powder
1 tbsp agave nectar

1 Cut the bananas into 2-cm/³/4-inch pieces. Place them in a freezer bag and freeze for 3 hours.

2 Put the frozen bananas in a food processor or blender. Add the cocoa powder and agave nectar and process until smooth. Scoop and serve immediately or refreeze for a firmer consistency.

BANANA BONUS

Bananas are high-energy fruit that are particularly loaded with fibre and potassium. They are considered to be effective in lowering blood pressure.

PER SERVING: 92 CALS | 0.8G FAT | 0.4G SAT FAT | 23.2G CARBS | 12.8G SUGARS | TRACE SALT | 3.3G FIBRE | 1.6G PROTEIN

WHOLEGRAIN DARK-CHOCOLATE BROWNIES

Who can resist a squidgy, just-warm chocolate brownie? This version has about half the butter and sugar of traditional brownies, but still has a deep, rich chocolatey flavour.

MAKES: 20 BROWNIES   PREP: 20 MINS
COOK: 25 MINS   COOL: 15 MINS

175 g/6 oz dates, stoned and chopped
125 ml/4 fl oz water
100 g/3½ oz plain chocolate with 70% cocoa,
broken into pieces
70 g/2½ oz unsalted butter
55 g/2 oz light muscovado sugar
25 g/1 oz unsweetened cocoa powder
25 g/1 oz wholemeal plain flour
1 tsp baking powder
2 eggs, beaten

1 Preheat the oven to 180°C/350°F/Gas Mark 4. Line a 20-cm/8-inch shallow square non-stick cake tin with a large square of baking paper, snipping into the corners diagonally then pressing the paper into the tin so that both the base and sides are lined.

2 Put the dates and water in a saucepan. Bring the water to the boil, cover, turn the heat down to medium-low and simmer for 5 minutes, or until the dates have softened. Add the chocolate, butter and sugar and stir until melted. Take the pan off the heat.

3 Sift the cocoa into a bowl, then mix in the flour and baking powder. Add the eggs and the flour mixture to the saucepan and stir until smooth. Pour the mixture into the prepared tin and spread it into an even layer. Bake for 18-20 minutes, or until well risen and the centre is only just set.

4 Leave to cool in the tin for 15 minutes. Lift the cake out of the tin, cut it into 20 brownies and peel off the paper.

ALSO TRY THIS...

Nut fans might like to toast 55 g/2 oz unblanched hazelnuts in a dry pan, then roughly chop them and stir half into the brownie mixture then sprinkle the rest over the top just before baking.

PER BROWNIE: 91.6 CALS | 5.7G FAT | 3.4G SAT FAT | 9.4G CARBS | 6.7G SUGARS | 0.2G SALT | 1.2G FIBRE | 1.7G PROTEIN

APPLE-SAUCE SPICED CUPCAKES

These lemony apple cupcakes are satisfying and wholesome, containing muscovado sugar and wholemeal flour.

MAKES: 12 CUPCAKES   PREP: 40 MINS
COOK: 1 HOUR 15 MINS   COOL: 30 MINS

3 dessert apples
finely grated zest and juice of 1 unwaxed lemon
85 g/3 oz wholemeal plain flour
85 g/3 oz brown rice flour
2 tsp baking powder
1/2 tsp ground mixed spice, plus extra to decorate
115 g/4 oz unsalted butter, softened and diced
115 g/4 oz light muscovado sugar
2 eggs, beaten
225 ml/8 fl oz crème fraîche

1 To make the apple sauce, peel, core and roughly chop two of the apples, then put them in a saucepan. Add the lemon zest and half the juice, cover and cook over a medium-low heat for 5–10 minutes, or until soft. Mash until smooth, then leave to cool. Preheat the oven to 180°C/350°F/Gas Mark 4.

2 Put 12 paper cases or squares of baking paper in a 12-hole muffin tin. Put the wholemeal and rice flours, baking powder and mixed spice in a small bowl and mix well.

3 Cream the butter and sugar together in a large bowl. Beat in alternate spoonfuls of the eggs and the flour mixture until it is all used up, then stir in 150 g/5½ oz apple sauce (reserve any remaining for another time).

4 Spoon the mixture into the paper cases. Bake for 15–18 minutes, or until well risen and the tops spring back when pressed with a fingertip. Leave to cool for 5 minutes, then transfer to a wire rack.

5 Line a baking sheet with baking paper. Put the rest of the lemon juice in a medium bowl. Thinly slice the remaining apple, toss it in the lemon juice, then arrange it on the prepared baking sheet. Reduce the oven temperature to 110°C/225°F/Gas Mark ¼ and cook the apple slices, turning once, for 30 45 minutes, or until just beginning to brown. Turn off the oven and leave the apples to cool inside it. Lift off the slices with a palette knife and cut them in half.

6 Top each cupcake with a spoonful of crème fraîche, sprinkle with mixed spice and put two apple slice halves on top.

MAKE IT SIMPLE

These cakes are great without any decoration, and make a healthy addition to the kids' school lunchboxes.

PER CAKE: 224 CALS | 12.8G FAT | 7.5G SAT FAT | 25.6G CARBS | 13.9G SUGARS | 0.6G SALT | 1.9G FIBRE | 3.2G PROTEIN

WHOLEWHEAT MUFFINS

*These sweet, flavour-packed muffins are crammed with healthy ingredients,
so you can enjoy them with none of the guilt you might feel if eating an ordinary muffin.*

MAKES: 10 MUFFINS   PREP: 15 MINS   COOK: 30 MINS

225 g/8 oz wholemeal self-raising flour
2 tsp baking powder
25 g/1 oz light muscovado sugar
100 g/3½ oz dried apricots, finely chopped
1 banana, peeled
1 tbsp freshly squeezed orange juice
1 tsp finely grated orange zest
300 ml/10 fl oz milk
1 egg, beaten
3 tbsp virgin olive oil
2 tbsp porridge oats
honey or maple syrup, to serve

1 Preheat the oven to 200°C/400°F/Gas Mark 6. Put 10 paper muffin cases in a muffin tray.

2 Sift the flour and baking powder into a bowl, adding any husks that remain in the sieve. Stir in the sugar and apricots.

3 Put the banana and orange juice in a separate bowl and mash. Add the orange zest, milk, egg and oil, then mix well.

4 Make a well in the centre of the flour mixture. Pour the banana mixture into the hole and mix well. Spoon the batter into the paper cases.

5 Sprinkle each muffin with a few porridge oats. Bake for 25–30 minutes, or until well risen and the tops spring back when pressed with a fingertip. Transfer to a wire rack. Serve warm, with a little honey or maple syrup.

WHOLEMEAL FLOUR

If you want to replace white flour with wholemeal flour in your recipes when baking at home, be sure to add a little more liquid.

PER MUFFIN: 173 CALS | 4.5G FAT | 0.7G SAT FAT | 25.6G CARBS | 9.5G SUGARS | 0.5G SALT | 2G FIBRE | 4.5G PROTEIN

RASPBERRY RICOTTA CHEESECAKE

Traditionally cheesecakes have a crushed biscuit base, but this granola-style base is packed with protein-filled nuts and cholesterol-lowering oats.

SERVES: 8   PREP: 40 MINS   COOK: 15 MINS
SOAK: 5 MINS   CHILL: 6 HOURS

25 g/1 oz unsalted butter
1 tbsp virgin olive oil, plus extra to grease
6 tbsp maple syrup, plus extra to serve
40 g/1^{1}/$_{2}$ oz porridge oats
40 g/1^{1}/$_{2}$ oz unblanched almonds, roughly chopped
40 g/1^{1}/$_{2}$ oz unblanched hazelnuts, roughly chopped

TOPPING

4 tbsp cold water
2^{1}/$_{2}$ tsp powdered gelatine
250 g/9 oz ricotta cheese
250 g/9 oz mascarpone cheese
250 g/9 oz natural yogurt
finely grated zest and juice of 1 unwaxed lemon, plus extra zest to decorate
150 g/5^{1}/$_{2}$ oz raspberries

1 To make the base, preheat the oven to 160°C/325°F/Gas Mark 3. Brush a 23-cm/9-inch diameter round non-stick springform tart tin with a little oil. Put the butter, oil and 2 tablespoons of maple syrup in a saucepan over a medium-low heat until the butter has melted. Remove the pan from the heat and stir in the oats and nuts.

2 Tip the mixture into the prepared tin and press down into an even layer with the back of a fork. Bake for 15 minutes, or until golden, then leave to cool.

3 To make the topping, spoon the water into a small heatproof bowl, then sprinkle the gelatine over the top, making sure all the powder is absorbed. Soak for 5 minutes. Place the bowl over a saucepan of gently simmering water until you have a clear liquid.

4 Put the ricotta, mascarpone and yogurt in a bowl, spoon in the remaining 4 tablespoons of maple syrup and whisk until smooth. Mix in the lemon zest and juice, then gradually whisk in the gelatine mixture. Add half the raspberries and crush them into the mixture with a fork.

5 Spoon the topping onto the base and smooth the surface, then sprinkle with the remaining raspberries. Cover the cheesecake and chill in the refrigerator for 4–6 hours, or until set.

6 To serve, run a knife around the edge of the tin, release the side and slide the cheesecake onto a serving plate. Decorate with the remaining lemon zest. To serve, cut into wedges and drizzle with extra maple syrup.

FREEZE IT!

This cheesecake can be frozen for up to two months. Wrap the tin in clingfilm, seal and label. Defrost in the refrigerator for four hours, then for one hour at room temperature.

PER SERVING: 389 CALS | 29.3G FAT | 14.3G SAT FAT | 22.9G CARBS | 14.1G SUGARS | 0.2G SALT | 3.2G FIBRE | 11G PROTEIN

HONEYED CARROT
AND PECAN SQUARES

This cake is packed with vitamin A-boosting carrots, vitamin B- and mineral-boosting wheatgerm and energy-boosting wholemeal flour.

MAKES: 15 SQUARES   PREP: 25 MINS   COOK: 35 MINS

3 eggs
150 ml/5 fl oz virgin olive oil
115 g/4 oz light muscovado sugar
5 tbsp set honey
175 g/6 oz wholemeal plain flour
4 tbsp wheatgerm
2 tsp baking powder
2 tsp ground ginger
grated zest of 1 orange, plus extra to decorate
1¼ tsp ground mixed spice
175 g/6 oz carrots, coarsely grated
55 g/2 oz pecan nuts, broken into pieces, plus extra to decorate

FROSTING
115 g/4 oz Greek-style natural yogurt
150 g/5½ oz cream cheese or mascarpone

1 Preheat the oven to 180°C/350°F/Gas Mark 4. Line a small non-stick roasting tin with a base measurement of 18 x 28 cm/7 x 11 inches with baking paper, snipping into the corners diagonally then pressing the paper into the tin so that both the base and sides are lined.

2 Crack the eggs into a large bowl, add the oil, sugar and 4 tablespoons of honey and whisk until smooth. Put the flour, wheatgerm and baking powder in a small bowl, then add the ginger, orange zest and 1 teaspoon of mixed spice and stir. Add the dry ingredients to the egg mixture and whisk again until smooth. Add the carrots and pecans and stir.

3 Spoon the mixture into the prepared tin and spread it into an even layer. Bake for 30–35 minutes, or until well risen and a skewer comes out cleanly when inserted into the centre of the cake.

4 Remove the cake from the tin, peel off the baking paper and turn out onto a wire rack. Leave to cool.

5 To make the frosting, put the yogurt, cream cheese and remaining 1 tablespoon of honey and ¼ teaspoon of mixed spice into a bowl and beat together until smooth. Spread the frosting over the cake, then sprinkle with extra pecans and orange zest. Cut it into 15 squares and serve.

ALSO TRY THIS...

Use 175 g/6 oz coarsely grated raw beetroot in place of the carrots.

PER SQUARE: 294 CALS | 20G FAT | 5.3G SAT FAT | 25.8G CARBS | 14.9G SUGARS | 0.5G SALT | 2.4G FIBRE | 5.3G PROTEIN

GINGER, NUT AND OAT BISCUITS

Biscuits warm from the oven make a great welcome for kids back from school or for guests. Keep the dough in the refrigerator and slice off biscuits, then bake for 15 minutes.

MAKES: 18 BISCUITS PREP: 30 MINS
CHILL: 30 MINS COOK: 15 MINS

175 g/6 oz unsalted butter, softened and diced, plus extra to grease
115 g/4 oz dark muscovado sugar
2.5–cm/1–inch piece fresh ginger, peeled and finely chopped
150 g/5^1/$_2$ oz wholemeal plain flour
85 g/3 oz porridge oats
70 g/2^1/$_2$ oz unblanched hazelnuts, roughly chopped
70 g/2^1/$_2$ oz unblanched almonds, roughly chopped

1 Place a sheet of baking paper about 30 cm/12 inches long on a work surface.

2 Cream the butter, sugar and ginger together in a large bowl. Gradually beat in the flour, then the oats and nuts, until you have a soft dough. Spoon the mixture into a 25–cm/10–inch line along the baking paper, then press it into a 5–cm/2–inch diameter roll. Wrap in the paper and chill in the refrigerator for 30 minutes, or up to three days.

3 Preheat the oven to 180°C/350°F/Gas Mark 4. Grease two baking sheets with butter. Unwrap the biscuit dough and slice off as many biscuits as you require. Arrange on the baking sheets, leaving a little space between each biscuit. Bake for 12–15 minutes, or until cracked and browned at the edges.

4 Leave the biscuits to cool for 5 minutes, then loosen and transfer them to a wire rack to cool completely.

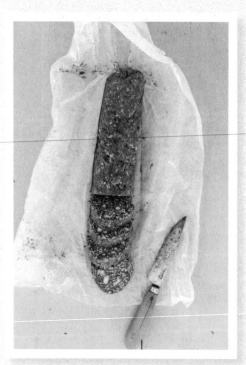

ALSO TRY THIS...

Try these biscuits with roughly chopped plain chocolate or dates and finely grated orange zest instead of the ginger and chopped nuts.

PER BISCUIT: 186 CALS | 12.7G FAT | 5.4G SAT FAT | 16.6G CARBS | 6.8G SUGARS | TRACE SALT | 2.2G FIBRE | 2.3G PROTEIN

STUFFED NECTARINES

This indulgent-tasting summer dessert is packed with vitamin C and fibre,
and takes just minutes to prepare.

SERVES: 4   PREP: 15 MINS   COOK: 10 MINS

4 tbsp Greek-style natural yogurt
finely grated zest of 1/2 orange
4 ripe nectarines or peaches, halved and stoned
140 g/5 oz blueberries
115 g/4 oz raspberries
150 ml/5 fl oz freshly squeezed orange juice
2 tsp runny honey
1 tbsp brandy (optional)

1 Preheat the oven to 180°C/350°F/Gas Mark 4. Put the yogurt and orange zest in a small bowl, cover and chill in the refrigerator while you make the rest of the dessert.

2 Put the nectarines in a shallow ovenproof dish. Fill the hollows left by the removal of the nectarine stones with a mixture of blueberries and raspberries. Put any extra berries around the edge.

3 Put the orange juice, honey and brandy, if using, in a small jug, mix well, then pour over the fruit. Bake for 10 minutes, or until hot.

4 Serve immediately with the orange yogurt.

BUYING FRUIT

Avoid under-ripe nectarines as it will
be difficult to remove the stones.

PER SERVING: 159 CALS | 2.7G FAT | 1.2 SAT FAT | 31.7G CARBS | 23G SUGARS | TRACE SALT | 5.4 FIBRE | 3.2G PROTEIN

CRUSTED CINNAMON ORANGES

Halved oranges, topped with cinnamon and sugar, will smell delicious as they grill, and are a simple way to end a meal – or even for breakfast.

SERVES: 4   PREP: 5 MINS   COOK: 5 MINS

4 large oranges, halved and pips discarded
1 tsp ground cinnamon
1 tbsp light muscovado sugar

1 Preheat the grill to high. Carefully cut the orange flesh away from the skin by cutting around the edge of the fruit with a sharp knife. Cut across the segments to loosen the flesh into bite-sized pieces that will then spoon out easily.

2 Arrange the orange halves, cut-side up, in a shallow, flameproof dish. Put the cinnamon and sugar in a small bowl, mix, then sprinkle over the oranges.

3 Grill for 3–5 minutes, or until the sugar has caramelised and is golden and bubbling. Serve immediately.

ALSO TRY THIS...

Top with natural yogurt mixed with honey for an extra-special treat.

PER SERVING: 88 CALS | 0.2G FAT | 0G SAT FAT | 20G CARBS | 20G SUGARS | TRACE SALT | 3.5G FIBRE | 1.5G PROTEIN

SPICED PLUM AND BLACKBERRY BRULEES

A fresh, fruity autumn compote lightly spiced with cinnamon, then topped with whipped cream and Greek-style natural yogurt for a no-bake brûlée custard – delicious!

SERVES:6   PREP: 15 MINS
CHILL: 30 MINS   COOK: 15 MINS

300 g/10½ oz plums, stoned and sliced
175 g/6 oz blackberries
2 tbsp water
¼ tsp ground cinnamon
5 tbsp light muscovado sugar
225 ml/8 fl oz double cream
225 g/8 oz Greek-style natural yogurt

1 Put the plums, blackberries and water in a saucepan, sprinkle over the cinnamon and 2 tablespoons of the sugar, then cover and cook over a medium–low heat for 10 minutes, or until just tender. Leave to cool.

2 Put the cream in a large bowl and whisk until soft swirls form, then fold in the yogurt.

3 Spoon the fruit and a little of the juice into six ovenproof 175-ml/6-fl oz ramekins or soufflé dishes. Dot teaspoons of the cream mixture over the top, then spread it into an even layer. Chill for at least 30 minutes.

4 Sprinkle the remaining 3 tablespoons of sugar over the tops of the dishes, then stand them in the base of the grill pan, pack ice around them to keep them cold and grill for 4–5 minutes, or until the sugar has dissolved and caramelised. Leave to cool for 2 minutes, then serve.

MAKE IT EASY

Caramelise the sugar at the very last minute with a cook's blowtorch instead of grilling.

PER SERVING: 310 CALS | 24G FAT | 15G SAT FAT | 21G CARBS | 21G SUGARS | TRACE SALT | 2.2G FIBRE | 4.9G PROTEIN

MANGO FRUITY CRUSH LOLLIES

These three-layered fruity, creamy treats are packed with colour, texture and flavour. The mango and strawberries work hand-in-hand with the vanilla.

MAKES: 8 ICE LOLLIES
PREP: 20 MINS   FREEZE: 8 HOURS

325 g/11¹/2 oz mango flesh
9 tbsp runny honey
300 ml/10 fl oz natural yogurt
2 tsp vanilla bean extract
300 g/10¹/2 oz strawberries, hulled

1 Put the mango in a blender or food processor and process to a purée. Transfer to a jug, add 3 tablespoons of honey and stir well.

2 Pour the mixture into 8 x 100 ml/3¹/2 fl oz ice lolly moulds. Freeze for 2 hours, or until firm.

3 When the mango mixture is frozen, put the yogurt, vanilla bean extract and 3 tablespoons of honey in a bowl and stir well. Spoon this over the frozen mango mixture. Insert the ice lolly sticks and freeze for 2–3 hours, or until firm.

4 When the vanilla mixture is frozen, put the strawberries and remaining 3 tablespoons of honey in a blender and process to a purée. Sieve out the seeds with a fine metal sieve. Pour this over the frozen vanilla mixture and freeze for 2–3 hours, or until firm.

5 To unmould the lollies, dip the frozen moulds into warm water for a few seconds and gently release the lollies while holding the sticks.

MMM, MANGO!

Mangoes contain a selection of vitamins and minerals, and are particularly rich in vitamin C and beta–carotene, which the body converts into vitamin A.

PER LOLLY: 141 CALS | 0.7G FAT | 0.3G SAT FAT | 33.3G CARBS | 31.7G SUGARS | TRACE SALT | 1.4G FIBRE | 2.5G PROTEIN

INDEX